Author: David Skidmore, University of Bath

ISBN: 0335204813

Price: £18.99

Please let me know if you have any queries. I look forward to receiving a copy of any review that you publish.

Yours sincerely

Malie Kluever
Product Manager
malie_kluever@mcgraw-hill.com

||||| OPEN UNIVERSITY PRESS

M c G r a w - H i l l E d u c a t i o n

MCGRAW-HILL HOUSE, SHOPPENHANGERS ROAD, MAIDENHEAD, SL6 2QL,
UNITED KINGDOM
Tel: +44 (0) 1628 502 500 Fax: +44 (0) 1628 770 224 Email: enquiries@openup.co.uk
www.openup.co.uk

19/07/2004

Dear Journal Reviewer

Book for Review

I enclose a copy of *Inclusion: The Dynamic of School Development* for review in your journal.

The book bridges the gap between theoretical discussions and the real attitudes and experiences of teachers and parents. It features case studies of inclusion initiatives in English secondary schools.

INCLUSION: THE DYNAMIC OF SCHOOL DEVELOPMENT

INCLUSIVE EDUCATION

Series Editors:

Gary Thomas, Chair in Education, Oxford Brookes University, and
Christine O'Hanlon, School of Education, University of East Anglia.

The movement towards inclusive education is gathering momentum throughout the world. But how is it realized in practice? The volumes within this series
will examine the arguments for inclusive schools and the evidence for the
success of inclusion. The intention behind the series is to fuse a discussion
about the ideals behind inclusion with the pictures of inclusion in practice.
The aim is to straddle the theory/practice divide, keeping in mind the strong
social and political principles behind the move to inclusion while observing
and noting the practical challenges to be met.

Current and forthcoming titles:

INCLUSION: THE DYNAMIC OF SCHOOL DEVELOPMENT

David Skidmore

Open University Press

Open University Press
McGraw-Hill Education
McGraw-Hill House
Shoppenhangers Road
Maidenhead
Berkshire
England
SL6 2QL

email: enquiries@openup.co.uk
world wide web: www.openup.co.uk

and Two Penn Plaza, New York, NY 10121-2289, USA

First published 2004

A catalogue record of this book is available from the British Library

ISBN 0 335 20481 3 (pb)   0 335 20482 1 (hb)

Library of Congress Cataloging-in-Publication Data
CIP data has been applied for

Typeset by RefineCatch Limited, Bungay, Suffolk
Printed in the UK by MPG Books Ltd, Bodmin, Cornwall

Dedication

For Dominic

Acknowledgements

I would like to thank the staff of Downland and Sealey Cove schools for making me welcome, and for giving up their time to help with my research. My particular thanks go to the two coordinators of learning support, for without their cooperation, this study would not have been possible.

I have benefited from discussions with many students and colleagues, who have helped to clarify my thinking even where we have not always agreed with one another. My particular thanks are due to Paul Croll for supervising my doctoral thesis, to Ian Copeland for acting as a critical friend and to Kevin Brehony for comradeship and the opportunity to discuss ideas.

Contents

Series editors' preface

'Inclusion' has become something of an international buzz-word. It's difficult to trace its provenance or the growth in its use over the last two decades, but what is certain is that it is now *de rigeur* for mission statements, political speeches and policy documents of all kinds. It has become a cliché – obligatory in the discourse of all right-thinking people.

The making of 'inclusion' into a cliché, inevitable as it perhaps is, is nevertheless disappointing, since it means that the word is often merely a filler in the conversation. It means that people can talk about 'inclusion' without really thinking about what they mean, merely to add a progressive gloss to what they are saying. Politicians who talk casually about the need for a more inclusive society know that they will be seen as open-minded and enlightened, and will be confident in the knowledge that all sorts of difficult practical questions can be circumvented. If this happens, and if there is insufficient thought about the nitty gritty mechanics (what the Fabians called 'gas and water' matters), those who do work hard for inclusion can easily be dismissed as peddling empty promises.

This series is dedicated to examining in detail some of the ideas which lie behind inclusive education. Inclusion, much more than 'integration' or 'mainstreaming', is embedded in a range of contexts – political and social as well as psychological and educational – and our aim in this series is to make some examination of these contexts. In providing a forum for discussion and critique we hope to provide the basis for a wider intellectual and practical foundation for more inclusive practice in schools and elsewhere.

In noting that inclusive education is indeed about more than simply 'integration', it is important to stress that inclusive education is really about extending the comprehensive ideal in education. Those who talk about it are therefore less concerned with children's supposed 'special educational needs' (and it is becoming increasingly difficult meaningfully to define what such needs are) and more concerned with developing an education system in which tolerance, diversity and equity are striven for. To aim for such developments is surely uncontentious; what is perhaps more controversial is the means by which this is done. There are many and varied ways of helping to develop more inclusive schools and the authors of this series look at some of these. While one focus in this has to be on the place and role of the special school, it is by no means the only focus: the thinking and practice which go on inside and outside schools may do much to exclude or marginalize children and the authors of this series try to give serious attention to such thinking and practice.

The books in this series therefore examine a range of matters: the knowledge of special education; the frames of analysis which have given legitimacy to such knowledge; the changing political mood which inspires a move to inclusion. In the context of all this, they also examine some new developments in inclusive thinking and practice inside and outside schools.

In *Inclusion: the Dynamic of School Development*, David Skidmore reveals how the real world of school responds to the initiatives of Government and LEAs. Two mainstream English secondary schools, Downland and Sealey Cove are creating more inclusive provision through restructuring initiatives. A case study approach is used to examine both situations on two levels. First the organizational structural level providing support for pupils with difficulties in learning is explored, and second the language used by teachers to discuss pupils, their difficulties and the schools' response to them is interpreted. The different discourses of teaching and learning diverge systematically along a number of dimensions. The nature of the relationship between the discourses shows the different connections between those involved and their divergent meanings and understandings.

The book exposes the consequences of recent pressures from the National Curriculum on schools, teachers and pupils. The traditions, ethos and general organization of the two schools chosen for the study illustrate how in specific school situations staff perceptions may lead to more favourable conditions for the reform of pedagogical thinking and institutional practice. It emphasizes the importance of the discourse of inclusion in teachers' professional development and its influence on curriculum issues, for example, the need for flexibility in the choice of teaching methods. Certain identifiable conditions outlined in the case study of Sealey Cove created a collaborative, proactive and inspirational school culture within a discourse of inclusion. However, in Downland school a discourse of deviance embedded in the view of the pupil as being deficient in some aspect of learning, had a strong influence on the reshaping of school policy and provision.

The evidence presented is compelling and convincing. The reality of the school cultures can be felt and almost experienced in the evidence and conversations presented. We can all relate to ideas, issues and opinions expressed by the participants.

The crucial point being made by Skidmore is that the inclusion discourse is challenging to the organizational status quo while the deviance discourse is used in defence of custom and practice. Yet it is the inclusion discourse which is necessary for the advance of true inclusive practice and the acceptance and promotion of student individuality and difference. The institutionalized ways that schools and teachers respond to human difference may be defined through restricted or flexible social interaction that can be learned and perpetuated. The dominant school discourse influences the teachers' attitudes and values and consequently their pupils' experiences and learning. Skidmore concludes that for a fully participatory education system to flourish, teachers' open and flexible discourse concerning reform of the curriculum, its presentation and the active participation of all students is critical for the success of educational inclusion.

Christine O'Hanlon
Gary Thomas

Preface

My brother, Dominic, was born on 6 January 1960. In 1964, our parents received a letter from the Director of the City Council's Education Department, which said that having considered the advice they had received from a doctor, the Local Education Authority had decided that Dominic was 'suffering from such a disability of mind as to make him unsuitable for education at school'. They proposed to record that decision and after that, the Council would not be able to admit him to any of their schools or send him to any other school.

In 1989, Dominic and our mother, Joan, wrote a book called *Time on My Hands*. Dominic had been confined to bed by a disabling back condition for much of the previous two years, and in this book he described the many hobbies and interests which helped to stop him getting bored while he had to stay indoors, including raising money for charity, reading and writing, and entertaining his friends and family. The book was completed just a few weeks before his death from a sudden chest infection in October of that year. In a postscript Joan (an experienced schoolteacher) explained how she helped Dominic write the book by acting as his secretary and co-author, writing down the gist of his ideas and comments in a style which she felt was appropriate to his ability; since he could read it back to her, she was satisfied that it was truly a joint effort.

How could someone capable as an adult of co-authoring a book be seen in childhood as unsuitable for education at school? Dominic was refused admission to school because he had Down's syndrome and what today would be called severe learning difficulties. Education policy in Britain has changed since 1964, and today children with Down's syndrome are not generally seen as unsuitable for education. Indeed increasingly, they and other children with learning difficulties and disabilities are educated in mainstream schools alongside their peers. This practice is often called 'inclusion', a term which has become something of a buzzword in discussions of education and social policy. Much of the debate, however, amounts to little more than the trading of abstract ideological positions, which has little connection with the reality of school practice and provision.

This book sets out to bridge the gap between theoretical discussions of the principle of inclusion and the real world of schooling. In Chapter 1, I review the main traditions of thinking in the research literature on the education of pupils with disabilities and difficulties in learning, identifying three main schools of thought, which I call the psycho-medical, the sociological and the organizational paradigms. Different as these are, I suggest that they share the common limitation of reductionism, that is they tend to explain a complex phenomenon in terms of a single factor. In Chapter 2, I update this map of the field by exploring an emerging tradition of research which adopts a critical perspective towards the education of pupils with difficulties and disabilities, but which avoids the reductionism of earlier work.

In Chapters 3 and 4, I seek to build on the strengths of this emerging tradition by presenting and interpreting evidence from two mainstream English secondary schools, which I call Downland and Sealey Cove, where initiatives were under way to introduce more inclusive forms of provision. In each school, I show that different groups of teachers thought about provision for pupils with difficulties in learning in contrasting ways, which carried very different implications for the development of the school. I also describe the different kinds of relationship which existed between the groups who held these contrasting outlooks, illustrating the complex, dynamic nature of the school development process.

In Chapter 5, on the basis of a comparison between the different perspectives in Downland and Sealey Cove, I put forward a theoretical model of pedagogical discourse, understood as an interconnected set of beliefs about education which combine to make up a working theory of schooling. I identify two contrasting forms of pedagogical discourse, which I term the discourse of deviance and the discourse of inclusion, differentiated along a series of dimensions (beliefs about educability, explanations of educational failure, strategies of learning support provision, theories of teaching expertise and implied model of the curriculum). I illustrate the dominant influence of the discourse of deviance on the history of education policy in the West during the twentieth century. I then seek to anchor the precepts of the discourse of inclusion in critical education theory, drawing particularly on Vygotsky's socio-cultural theory of the mind. In conclusion, I attempt to articulate the implications of this alternative vision of the relationship between education and society for education policy, pedagogy and the curriculum. If we accept an open-ended view of human educability, then it suggests that we need to work to overcome the processes of selection and differentiation which characterize schooling today, and work to create a unified system of comprehensive education built on the recognition that the experience of participating in a diverse learning community is necessary for the full development of each person's individual capabilities.

CHAPTER ONE

Traditions of thinking about learning difficulties

In this chapter, I will identify the major traditions of research into the education of pupils with difficulties in learning up to the early 1990s which can be
seen as paradigmatic, in the sense that they are characteristic of significant
bodies of work in the field. I will illustrate the methods and findings of these
traditions with reference to influential examples of each; and I will explicate
and critically evaluate the conceptualization of learning difficulties implied by
these traditions. I will argue that three major traditions of thinking or research
paradigms can be distinguished, viz. the psycho-medical, the sociological, and
the organizational paradigms. I do not suggest that these paradigms exhaust-
ively classify all writing in this field; nor that the categories are watertight; nor
that all writers operating within one paradigm agree upon how the education
system should respond to pupils with difficulties in learning. Rather, dis-
criminating between these paradigms can help us to orientate ourselves
towards significant bodies of existing work in the field. It also permits a range
of models to be distinguished which might be used to guide the design of
further research. I would suggest, however, these paradigms have a certain
substantive validity, inasmuch as each can be seen to draw upon a distinct
theoretical framework, whose origins lie in independent research in cognate
fields; typically, therefore, writers working within one of the paradigms hold
many elements of vocabulary, research design and reporting procedure in
common. Although my survey is not concerned to trace the historical development of these paradigms, it will be convenient to treat them in order of
approximate historical seniority (Clark et al. 1995b). In each case, however,
the focus will be on recent influential work exemplifying the characteristics
of the paradigm in question.

The psycho-medical paradigm

The historical roots of research into learning difficulties lie in writing from the medical and psychological traditions (Burt 1937; Schonell 1942). Although, as the discussion below will indicate, writing which draws on other conceptual frameworks has come to occupy a position in the foreground of this field, work which owes its primary allegiance to the psycho-medical paradigm continues to exert a strong influence. Work in this paradigm conceptualizes difficulties in learning as arising from deficits in the neurological or psychological make-up of the child, analogous to an illness or medical condition; in the US literature on learning disabilities, this is quite explicit, in the form of the 'minimal brain dysfunction' hypothesis, which ascribes difficulties in learning to otherwise undetected cortical lesions (Coles 1987). Much effort by writers in this paradigm is bent towards refining screening instruments designed to assist in the diagnosis of the supposed syndrome or condition, and the interventions prescribed tend to be quasi-clinical in character. Explicit discussion of the implications for teachers' classroom practice, though by no means entirely absent, is by contrast less prominent in this paradigm than is the case for the organizational and sociological paradigms. These writers adopt a positivist epistemological stance, using a writing style replete with the terminology of experimental science; commonly, published articles are structured as scientific reports on the empirical testing of hypotheses by means of field trials or clinical trials of interventions or diagnostic instruments. The number of putative syndromes identified by this paradigm is large and constantly growing. For the present purpose, I will illustrate its qualities by examining recently-published work on attention deficit disorder (including hyperactivity), a category of learning difficulty which is held to be relatively common, and has a direct bearing on provision in mainstream schools.

From its origins in studies of 'hyperkinesis' in the 1960s, the syndrome of Attention Deficit Disorder (ADD) was elevated to official status in 1980 by its inclusion in the *Diagnostic and Statistical Manual for Mental Disorders* (DSM) compiled by the American Psychiatric Association. It has been applied, along with closely associated terms such as hyperactivity, to identify that group of children whose behaviour in school persistently fails to conform to the norms of the orderly classroom, and whose learning and attainments are thereby impaired.

The internationally reputed American journal *Exceptional Children* dedicated an entire special issue to discussion of this syndrome (vol. 60, no. 2, 1993). The sequence of headline articles falls neatly into the structure of the psycho-medical approach to learning difficulties: diagnosis, neurological causation, and clinical intervention (Dykman and Ackerman 1993; McBurnett et al. 1993; Riccio et al. 1993). McBurnett et al. are concerned to demonstrate the 'increased validity and reliability' of the revised diagnostic criteria, a function, they claim, of the greater number of 'symptoms' required to be present before a diagnosis of ADD is made. Riccio et al. go on to review the various neurological models – based on supposed anatomical, chemical or physiological dysfunctions – which have been proposed in the aetiology of ADD. Finally,

Dykman and Ackerman identify three behavioural subtypes of ADD: without hyperactivity; with hyperactivity; and with hyperactivity and aggression. They go on to argue the need for an even further refined system of categorization, and for the identification of 'biological markers' (for example adrenalin secretion, salivation), before advocating the use of drugs to control the aggressive behaviour of children with ADD, concluding:

> Teachers and counselors . . . should find the medicated defiant/aggressive child more open to suggestions regarding socially acceptable ways to handle irritation and frustration.
>
> (1993: 193)

This series of articles epitomizes those features of research conducted in the psycho-medical paradigm which have led many educators to question this approach. Subtypes proliferate, and the pursuit of ever finer systems of categorization comes to be seen as an end in itself. The validity of a neurological model of causation is assumed a priori, in spite of the frank admission of 'the inability [of researchers] to map behavioral descriptors onto relevant neurologic components' (Riccio et al. 1993). Explicit discussion of the implications of these theories for educational interventions is almost entirely absent. Finally, the practice of drugging defiant children to make them more compliant is casually condoned as if the ethics of such a form of intervention required no further consideration. These points are echoed by critics who question the validity of ADD as a disability category, note the lack of evidence to substantiate a biological aetiology and report that students identified as ADD cannot necessarily be regarded as academic underachievers (Reid et al. 1993; Reid et al. 1994). Their verdict on the influence of the psycho-medical paradigm in this instance is damning:

> strict adherence to the medical/psychiatric perspective of ADHD [Attention Deficit Hyperactivity Disorder] has helped to obfuscate efforts to examine gaps in the knowledge base, as well as empirical and logical flaws in the assumptions underlying advocates' arguments.
>
> (Reid et al. 1993: 209)

Strengths and weaknesses of the psycho-medical paradigm

Any critique of writing about education in the psycho-medical paradigm must start from the recognition that there is a recurrent incidence of conditions in the general population which may affect pupils' learning and for which an organic basis is uncontroversial, for example Down's syndrome. There are other forms of disability, such as autism, where the case for physical causation is less certain, but which are known to be lifelong, and may be associated with communication disorders which are so severe that few would contest the need for further research within the conceptual framework of psychology.

Given its long historical roots, and the undoubted existence of such psychological and medical conditions, it is likely that research into learning difficulties in the psycho-medical paradigm will continue to be conducted, that it will continue to exert an influence on the wider field, and that some of its findings will be found to be of use in the education of pupils who are affected by conditions which are generally recognized to have an organic basis. The difficulty arises when illicit attempts are made to apply this framework to an infinitely-extensible set of putative syndromes or disorders for which reliable evidence of a neurological or organic basis is lacking, and where 'diagnosis' rests on value-laden, culturally-specific judgements about behavioural or cognitive norms. In the case of ADD, it is arguable that the scientistic discourse of positivism and the rhetorical stance of authoritative objectivity which it engenders have been deployed to disseminate a biological determinist hypothesis for which empirical evidence is wanting, and to legitimize the practice of drugging defiant children into docility, using stimulants whose long-term side effects are unknown, in the service of a tacit project of social control.

Historically, dissatisfaction with the more questionable influences of the psycho-medical paradigm has caused researchers in the field of learning difficulties to look to alternative conceptual frameworks to guide their inquiries. First among these has been research in the sociological paradigm.

The sociological paradigm

During the 1980s, a strand of sociologically-oriented research into special education emerged and came to assume an important position in the field. It has been particularly well-represented in work from the UK, and its influence remains significant. Seminal works in this paradigm include Tomlinson's ground-breaking analysis of special education (Tomlinson 1982), and Bines's research into the development of the role of the remedial teacher into the Special Needs Coordinator (Bines 1986). Significant contributions can also be found in the collections edited by Barton and Tomlinson (Barton and Tomlinson 1981, 1984b; Barton 1988).

It would be a mistake to imply that a single undifferentiated perspective unites all these works. Differing sociological traditions are drawn on by the various authors, some, for instance, subscribing to the theoretical framework of symbolic interactionism, deriving ultimately from Mead (for example Bogdan & Kugelmass 1984). However, the dominant perspective found among these writers can be described as a form of structuralist or neo-Marxist sociology. Taking over the theory of cultural reproduction from the general sociology of education, they apply it to the case of special education, developing and modifying its conceptual framework in the process. This results in an analysis of special education as a sorting mechanism contributing to the reproduction of existing social inequalities by syphoning off a proportion of the school population and assigning them to an alternative, lower-status educational track.

Various formulations of this conceptualization can be found in the literature. Tomlinson, for instance, deploys the metaphor of a 'safety valve'

(Tomlinson 1982) to describe the function of the special school system, referring to the way in which its existence allows troublesome and disruptive children to be removed from the mainstream system, which is thereby permitted
to continue undisturbed in its task of delivering an unreconstructed academic
curriculum to the majority. In a similar vein, Carrier (Carrier 1984) describes
special education as a mechanism for differentiating and allocating children to
different educational treatments. Like Tomlinson, he connects its emergence
historically to the development of mass public education:

> special education as a significant differentiating and allocating device is
> not a random occurrence, but appears only when mass education occurs
> in conjunction with an egalitarian ideology.
>
> (1984: 60)

This conceptualization marks a sharp break with the hypothesis of learning
difficulties as arising from neurological deficits inherent in the student which
typifies research in the psycho-medical paradigm. A shift away from this conceptualization was already to be found in the language of the Warnock Report
(DES 1978) and the succeeding Education Act (1981), which abolished the ten
existing statutory categories of handicap and introduced in their place the
concept of special educational needs. However, the later sociological writings
of Tomlinson and others (Tomlinson 1985) question whether this change in
terminology masks a practice of stratification which continues to determine
children's educational careers by assigning to them an identity defined by an
administrative label.

Strengths and weaknesses of the sociological paradigm

Perhaps the major achievement of work conducted within this paradigm is its
sustained critique of what Tomlinson calls the 'ideology of benevolent
humanitarianism' (Tomlinson 1982) which had for a long time been dominant in the field of special education. In the aftermath of this critique, it is no
longer possible to assume an a priori consensus around the idea that children
deemed to have difficulties in learning should be segregated from others and
subject to an alternative, lower-status form of educational provision. It may
also be judged to have had a direct impact on practice in sensitizing practitioners to the potentially damaging effects of attaching negative diagnostic
labels to pupils. Further, it has brought into the arena of debate the issue of the
co-existence of two separate school systems, the mainstream and the special.
Finally, although articulated mainly in the context of an inquiry into the
relationship between the special and mainstream sectors, the general principles of this critique have clear implications for the question of the treatment
of children with difficulties in learning within ordinary schools; for example,
whether they should be taught in withdrawal classes, or in the mainstream.

Against these achievements, however, it is necessary to note that much writing in this paradigm is marred by a tendency towards abstract, hypothetical
argument. Too often, writers take over concepts from general sociological
theory and argue for their applicability to the field of special education, but

neglect to support their point with empirical evidence; such as, for example, Freeman's discussion of the concept of social competence (Freeman 1988), or Bart's discussion of deviance (Bart 1984). At the extreme, this strain approaches polemic or, at any rate, the reasoned assertion of value positions founded on (at best) anecdotal evidence. Of course, this form of writing has its place, and may serve an important purpose when fundamental educational principles are at stake, but as research it is always open to the criticism of exceptionalism, in other words that its case is built on unrepresentative evidence.

Furthermore, writing in this paradigm tends to treat the 'sorting' function of special education as an automatic, mechanistic process, as if children arrived at one end of a conveyor belt and issued from the other, neatly allocated to their appropriate track, in a smooth, uninterrupted stream. Some studies, for example, lay great stress on the asymmetry of power relationships between professionals and parents (Tomlinson 1985; Wood 1988); but an asymmetrical relationship may nevertheless be contested, and it is not the case that professionals always have their way in deciding the form of schooling a child is to receive, nor indeed that the professionals always agree amongst themselves. Likewise, in their enthusiasm to demonstrate the continued operation of the sorting process despite apparent changes in the education system, some commentators tend to conflate very different policy regimes. This tendency is found, for instance, in Barton and Tomlinson's critique of the integration movement following the Warnock Report (Barton and Tomlinson 1984a) for its 'romanticism' in ignoring the inequalities endemic to schooling. Inequalities may indeed be endemic to schooling, but it is simplistic to suggest that there was no qualitative difference between the inequalities endemic to the regime of the 1944 Education Act, with its tripartite system of schools and ten statutory categories of handicap, and the inequalities endemic to the regime of the 1981 Act, with a system of comprehensive schools and the notion of a continuum of special educational needs.

Finally, early writing in this paradigm tends to neglect the need to articulate a coherent alternative to the state of affairs which it criticizes. This is particularly true of Tomlinson's work (Tomlinson 1982), which is pervaded by a sense of fatalism. There is some evidence, however, that recent work influenced by the tradition of sociological critique has begun to formulate a more explicit vision of alternative forms of policy and provision: compare the case made by Oliver (Oliver 1992) for the disabled to engage in a process of political struggle to create a more inclusive education system.

It is clear that the influence of the sociological paradigm on research in the field of special education remains strong. The need for policy analysis and critique, always strong elements in this tradition of writing, is unlikely to diminish in a period characterized by the major revision of special education policy brought about by the Code of Practice (DFE 1994a; DFES 2001), and extended by the New Labour Government's official commitment to the principles of inclusion (DFEE 1997, 1998) and disability rights in education (DRC 2002). We must hope that such critique will be informed by a greater recognition of the need to substantiate theoretical analysis with empirical evidence than has often been the case in the past. In the meantime, a third tradition of research into learning difficulties has arisen in recent years, in part as a reaction to the weaknesses of the sociological paradigm described above, viz. its tendency to abstraction, its application of undigested sociological concepts, and its deterministic perspective. This third paradigm draws on theoretical concepts formulated in the context of organizational research, and on other branches of educational research, notably the literatures on school effectiveness, school restructuring and school improvement.

The organizational paradigm

Beginning in the US in the late 1980s, a third tradition of research into learning difficulties emerged, which has recently come to assume a position of dominance in the field. The organizational paradigm sees difficulties in learning as arising from deficiencies in the way in which schools are currently organized; concomitantly, the solution advocated is to restructure schools to remove these deficiencies. Various formulations of this position are found in the literature which draw on different conceptual frameworks; consequently, the model of the reformed school put forward varies in detail from one contribution to another. Nevertheless, they are united in the conviction that a properly-implemented policy of school restructuring will produce a system of schooling which is better adapted to meeting the educational needs of all pupils, and which will therefore eliminate or reduce to a minimum the problem of students who fail to fulfil their learning potential in the formal education system. Although it is rarely made explicit, these authors can be seen as operating within a broadly functionalist perspective, which sees schools as more or less successful agents for socializing students into the skills, behaviours and values required by existing society. Three major variants of the school restructuring proposal are briefly described below: the adhocratic school, the heterogeneous school and the school which is effective for all students.

Drawing on the work of Mintzberg in the field of organization theory (Miller and Mintzberg 1983), Skrtic analyses schools as 'professional bureaucracies' in which teachers work in relative isolation from one another, and tend to fit the needs of pupils to their repertoire of skills, rather than adopting innovative solutions to the varying needs of students. Students with special needs are thus seen as 'artefacts of the traditional curriculum.' Skrtic puts forward the case for a reconfiguration of schools as 'adhocracies,' marked among other features by greater use of collaborative teamwork and the continuous coordination of work through informal communication (Skrtic 1991a, 1991b). Citing evidence from programmes of school restructuring, Villa and Thousand propose that schools should be reformed to 'accommodate for greater student variance,' that is to cater adequately for the educational needs of all students in the local community, including students with severe behaviour disorders and physical and sensory impairments who would previously have attended a separate special school. This model is termed the 'zero reject' or heterogeneous school (Thousand and Villa 1991; Villa et al. 1992). Drawing on the findings of research into school effectiveness, Ainscow (echoing Skrtic) argues that pupils experiencing difficulties should be seen as 'indicators of the need for institutional reform,' and suggests that schools which exhibit the characteristics identified in the effectiveness literature will be similarly successful in promoting the learning of all students, including those with special needs (Ainscow 1991a, 1991b, 1993). The findings of school effectiveness research thus furnish a model for the restructuring of schools which will minimize the incidence of learning difficulties.

These examples by no means exhaust the restructuring proposals which have been put forward. Others include: the refashioned mainstream (Gartner and Lipsky 1987, 1989); the adaptive learning environment (Wang 1991); the quality school (Glasser 1992); and school renewal as cultural change (Joyce et al. 1991). Though their terminology varies, these proposals share the common conceptualization of difficulties in learning noted above, that is that they are caused by pathologies in the way schools are currently organized, and that they can be overcome by reforming schools as organizations. There is presently a convergence of these views around the notion of the 'inclusive school,' which, its advocates suggest, would be adapted to respond to the full diversity of learning needs found in the student population; in this model, no group would be identified as 'special' and requiring a qualitatively different form of educational provision (Clark et al. 1995a). The inclusive schools movement is not without its critics, some portraying it as an extremist group whose radicalism will alienate those working in general education (Fuchs and Fuchs 1994), others casting doubt on the assumption that the effective school will be equally successful in promoting the learning of all pupils (Reynolds 1995). Nonetheless, there can be no doubt that the organizational paradigm currently commands widespread allegiance in the field of research into the education of pupils with disabilities and learning difficulties; from the point of view of theory development, its influence at present seems dominant.

Strengths and weaknesses of the organizational paradigm

Writing in the organizational paradigm has made a significant contribution to the understanding of how students come to have difficulties in learning by drawing attention to the role of school- and classroom-level variables – factors which lie within the power of educators to affect, and which (there is good evidence to suppose) are implicated in students' learning or failure to learn. By comparison, both the pupil-deficit conceptualization of learning difficulties associated with the psycho-medical paradigm, and the sociological conceptualization of learning difficulties as arising from macro-level processes of sorting and differentiation, had tended to underestimate the significance of these factors. In addition, some empirical evidence has been presented of school restructuring programmes which appear to be successful in promoting the social integration of students identified as having special needs, and which do not have an adverse impact on learning outcomes, and may be associated with improved attainment. (In spite of the author's anti-integrationist sentiments, this is the only conclusion that can be drawn from the review of research presented by Hornby (Hornby 1992).)

There are, however, a number of issues surrounding the conceptualization of learning difficulties offered by the organizational paradigm which remain unresolved. Foremost among these is its propensity to analyse the internal organizational characteristics of the school in isolation, that is to the exclusion of any other factors which may be implicated in the creation of difficulties in learning. Although some of these studies examine the effects of a variety of teaching strategies such as cooperative group learning, individualized instruction, and collaborative staff teams (Ainscow 1991b; Villa and Thousand 1992), the paradigm tends to operate with an image of the school as an organization which is globally effective or ineffective, inclusive or exclusive, heterogeneous or homogeneous, and neglects to investigate the individual interactions between teacher and student, or student and student, through which learning takes place. It is still weaker in integrating the impact of macro-level forces, such as national education policy, showing a tendency to suppress these altogether from the realm of inquiry. Writers also tend to adopt theoretical models or reported empirical findings which have been developed in other fields and assume that they can be applied unproblematically to the case of provision for pupils with learning difficulties. The theoretical model of the adhocratic configuration adopted by Skrtic, for instance, was developed by writers concerned to analyse the behaviour of large-scale industrial and state enterprises; and the school effectiveness studies from which Ainscow draws his list of key features were only tangentially concerned with special needs provision. Finally, there is a serious weakness in the understanding of organizational change displayed in the paradigm. Where writers address this question, they seem incapable of theorizing the process except in terms of a contest between visionary leaders and neurotic resistors (Joyce et al. 1991; Reynolds 1991; Villa and Thousand 1992). This is surely to prejudge the issue, and with such a simplistic understanding of the complex process of organizational development, it is scarcely surprising that some of the reported attempts to improve schools end in failure (Reynolds 1991). In spite of these weaknesses, a number of factors seem destined to secure a continued audience for the restructuring proposals put forward by writers in the organizational paradigm, viz.: the pragmatic focus of the paradigm on school-level factors which are amenable to practitioner influence; the articulation between this paradigm and other fashionable currents of educational research; and the assurance offered by the paradigm that a final solution to the enduring problem of educational underachievement is at hand, without the need for extra resources to be invested. For these reasons, it seems likely that this paradigm will continue to command the attention of researchers in the field, and that its findings will continue to have an impact on practitioners.

Mapping the field

In the foregoing, selective survey of research in the field of the education of pupils with disabilities and learning difficulties, I have suggested that it is possible to discern three major currents of writing, viz. the psycho-medical, the sociological and the organizational paradigms. Their principal character-istics were illustrated by a critical discussion of significant examples. I argued that each paradigm drew on a distinctive theoretical framework, operating with its own implied epistemology and characteristic level of focus, positing a different model of the causation of learning difficulties, and proposing a correspondingly different form of intervention. A summary of these distinctions is set forth in Table 1.1.

It is important to stress once again that I am not suggesting that identifying these paradigms permits all research in this field to be uniquely and exhaust-ively classified. Nevertheless, I have put forward evidence in the course of my

Table 1.1 The three major paradigms of research into the education of pupils with difficulties in learning

Paradigm	Epistemology	Level of focus	Model of causation	Form of intervention proposed
Psycho-medical	Positivist	Micro (individual)	Learning difficulties arise from deficits within the individual pupil	Diagnostic testing and quasi-clinical remediation
Sociological	Structuralist	Macro (societal)	Learning difficulties arise from the reproduction of structural inequalities in society through processes of sorting and tracking	Root and branch political reform of the education system to remove inequitable practices
Organizational	Functionalist	Meso (institutional)	Learning difficulties arise from deficiencies in the ways in which schools are currently organized	Programme of school restructuring to eliminate organizational deficiencies

survey to show that the conceptualizations associated with each paradigm exert a continued and significant influence on the discourse of the field, and on the design of research projects that come to be conducted. The relative influence of each paradigm no doubt varies, but, although they have emerged in the approximate order set out above, it would be wrong to think that one paradigm has succeeded or replaced its predecessors; rather, the field of research into learning difficulties has diversified and grown in complexity over time, with each paradigm continuing to attract contemporary adherents.

My analysis of the three paradigms has also brought to light certain limitations inherent in each. We have seen, for example, the tendency within the psycho-medical paradigm to extend an approach derived from the study of conditions with a known biological basis to cases where evidence for such a basis is weak or absent; the deterministic bias of writing within the sociological paradigm; and the exclusive focus of the organizational paradigm on structural features of the school as an institution. In general, I would argue that the three paradigms share the common fault of *reductionism*, that is the tendency to explain an intrinsically complex phenomenon in terms of a single, uni-directional model of causation, and (concomitantly) to propose a single form of intervention as a complete and adequate solution to the problem. Learning difficulties are conceptualized as the product of factors located within the individual, *or* society at large, *or* the school, but the possibility of interaction between factors operating at different levels of analysis is overlooked.

After proposing this map of the field on the basis of a survey of work up to the early 1990s, in the next chapter I will proceed to examine developments during the 1990s, beginning with the major revision of Government guidance on special educational needs in England and Wales. I will then explore evidence of continuities and developments within the established research paradigms, followed by a discussion of an emerging body of work which adopts a critical perspective towards current policy and practice in this area, but which avoids some of the weaknesses characteristic of work within the established traditions. I will summarize the state of contemporary educational research in the field of learning difficulties and identify a gap in the existing work. This gap provides the rationale for the study of the process of school development which is described in the succeeding chapters.

CHAPTER TWO

Developing inclusive schools: theory and evidence

The map of the field set out in Chapter 1 was drawn on the basis of a survey of influential work published mainly in the 1980s and 1990s. In this chapter, I will ask how well the 'map' stands up today, and what changes or qualifications need to be made to the picture presented above, in the light of an examination of relevant policy developments, and a discussion of a number of more recent works which have contributed to the development of thinking in the field.

Developments in education policy: The Code of Practice

The major policy development in the field of special needs education in England and Wales in the 1990s was the introduction, as a consequence of the 1993 Education Act, of the *Code of Practice on the Identification and Assessment of Special Educational Needs*. This was replaced by a revised version which was issued in 2001, coming into effect in January 2002 (DFES 2001). The legal status of the Code is analogous to that of the Highway Code: whilst it does not itself form a part of statute law, all those affected by it are obliged to 'have regard' to it:

> They must not ignore it. That means that whenever settings, schools and LEAs decide how to exercise their functions relating to children with special educational needs, and whenever the health services and social services help to settings, schools and LEAs in this, those bodies must consider what the Code says.
>
> (DFES 2001, Foreword: 5)

In England and Wales, the Code defines the essential framework of Government guidance on the treatment of children with special educational needs within which schools, LEAs and other agencies must work.

When it was first introduced, initial responses to the Code often centred upon concerns about the increased workload for teachers, and especially Special Educational Needs Coordinators, implied by the introduction of Individual Education Plans (IEPs) and regular progress reviews of all children on the school's Special Educational Needs register, including those without statements (I.C. Copeland 1997); against this, some commentators welcomed the high profile given to special needs provision in schools as a consequence of the Code, correcting the relative neglect of this issue in the major educational reforms introduced by the 1988 Education Act, particularly in relation to the National Curriculum (compare Clark et al. 1997). Relatively little attention, however, has been paid to the whole way of thinking about pupils' difficulties in learning upon which the approach of the Code is built, the assumptions and presuppositions which it embodies about the nature of these difficulties, and the way in which teachers and others should respond to them.

A number of 'fundamental principles' are set out in the introduction to the Code (DFES 2001, 1: 5), which include:

- the special educational needs of children will normally be met in mainstream schools and settings;
- the views of the child should be sought and taken into account;
- parents have a vital role to play in supporting their child's education;
- children with special educational needs should be offered full access to a broad, balanced and relevant education.

There is some continuity between the thinking which informs the Code and the central documents which defined the previous policy regime in special needs education (the Warnock Report (DES 1978) and the 1981 Education Act) in the use of the concept of a 'continuum' of needs and provision (DFES 2001, 6: 22), as there is in the conditional endorsement of a policy of integration. On the question of parents of children with special educational needs, whilst they had the right to be consulted under previous legislation, the Code considerably extended and strengthened their rights vis-à-vis the other partners in the process (especially schools and LEAs), for instance in the requirement for LEAs to make parent partnership services available, the introduction of an Independent Parental Supporter, who can act as an adviser during the statutory assessment process; and through the setting up of the Special Educational Needs Tribunal to determine appeals by parents against LEA decisions on assessments and statements. The principle of access to a broad common curriculum represents a significant departure from the previous legislative regime. Whilst the Warnock Report (DES 1978) famously held that 'The purpose of education for all children is the same; the goals are the same' (DFES 2001, 1: 4), the 1981 Education Act had little specific to say about the curriculum, and the Code's explicit endorsement of the principle of a common curriculum for all marks a new policy development in the field of special needs education. If we consider these principles in their totality, however, we can see that they are articulated at a high level of generality; to explore further the 'philosophy' of special needs education embodied in the Code, it is necessary to examine the mechanisms for identification and assessment which it recommends.

The Code recommends that schools should adopt a 'graduated response' to children's special educational needs. Under 'School Action', if a pupil fails to make progress despite the usual differentiation of the curriculum, then additional intervention, including an Individual Educational Plan, should be coordinated by the Special Educational Needs Coordinator (DFES 2001, 6: 50). If the pupil still fails to make the expected progress, then the school may request help from external services – known as 'School Action Plus' (6: 62). As a preamble to these additional intervention procedures, the Code states:

> Effective management, school ethos and the learning environment, curricular, disciplinary and pastoral arrangements can help prevent some special educational needs arising, and minimise others. Differentiation of learning activities . . . will help schools to meet the learning needs of all pupils. Schools should not assume that pupils' learning difficulties always result solely, or even mainly, from problems within the young person. Pupils' rates of progress can sometimes depend on what or how they are taught. A school's own practices make a difference – for good or ill.
>
> (6: 18)

Taken in isolation, this statement epitomizes the standpoint of the 'organizational paradigm' of research into learning difficulties which was described in Chapter 1, which ascribes difficulties in learning to deficiencies in school organization; certainly, the tradition has influenced the language of the Code at this point. Is the Code, then, a revision of special needs policy to bring it into line with the findings of this line of inquiry? To answer this question, this passing reference to school organization needs to be situated in the context of the machinery of identification, assessment and review which the Code sets out. If we look, for instance, for an operational definition of the terms 'special educational need' and 'learning difficulty', we find the following citation from the 1996 Education Act (1: 3; original emphases):

> Children have *special educational needs* if they have a *learning difficulty* which calls for *special educational provision* to be made for them.
>   Children have a *learning difficulty* if they:
> (a) have a significantly greater difficulty in learning than the majority of children of the same age;
> (b) have a disability which either prevents or hinders the child from making use of educational facilities of a kind provided for children of the same age in schools within the area of the local education authority;
> (c) are under compulsory school age and fall within the definition at (a) or (b) above or would do if special educational provision was not made for them.

This is a re-enactment of the legal definition first introduced in the 1981 Education Act, and exhibits the same circularity that was present in that legislation: 'special educational needs' are defined in terms of a 'learning difficulty', which is in turn defined in terms of a requirement for 'special educational provision', and in terms of a 'difficulty in learning' (determined normatively by comparison with the child's peer group). Although there is a reference to provision, changeable features of school organization do not feature in the definition; rather, a local norm of educational provision is presumed, and a child is seen as having special needs if he or she requires provision which is 'additional to, or otherwise different from' (DFES 2001, 1: 3) this norm. The legal definition of special educational needs, then, contains no recognition that these needs may arise because the norm of available provision is inadequate.

The concrete procedures set out in the Code (in Chapter 4 for early education settings, 5 for primary schools, and 6 for secondary schools) are largely concerned with regulating the process of identifying, assessing and reviewing the needs of individual children with difficulties. The curriculum is encompassed in the mechanism of the Individual Education Plan (IEP), which is actuated at the 'School Action' phase of assessment, and should set out the short-term targets set for or by the pupil, teaching strategies, provision, a date for review, success or exit criteria and outcomes. The revised Code places a stronger emphasis on pupil participation than its predecessor, but the vocabulary of targets and individualized intervention still seems to carry echoes of the 'behavioural objectives' school of pedagogy, popularized originally in the work of Bloom and colleagues (Bloom 1956), which was influenced by the behaviourist theory of learning formulated by Skinner (Skinner 1957). In any event, the perspective on educational provision which is encapsulated in the mechanism of the IEP is, by definition, a highly individualized approach, in which the development of a school's response to the difficulties experienced by pupils is seen as the aggregate outcome of a multitude of independent interventions made on a case-by-case basis.

A similar equivocation over diagnosis and intervention may be detected in the Code's guidance on the statutory assessment of special educational needs, the formal process in which primary responsibility for coordinating the assessment process passes from the school to the LEA, and which may result in the issuing of a statement of special educational needs. Discussing the evidence to be considered when deciding whether to make a statutory assessment, the Code advises:

> LEAs will always require evidence of the child's academic attainment in all areas of learning. . . .
>
> However, academic attainment is not in itself sufficient for LEAs to conclude that a statutory assessment is or is not necessary. An individual child's attainment must always be understood in the context of the attainments of the child's peers, the child's rate of progress over time and, where appropriate, expectations of the child's performance. A child's apparently weak performance may, on examination of the evidence, be attributable to wider factors associated with the school's organisation.
>
> (7: 38–9)

Once again, there is a clear formal recognition that difficulties in learning may be the result of deficiencies in the school rather than the deficits of the child.

However, the Code continues 'Nonetheless, attainment is the essential starting point when considering the evidence' (7: 40). Having first acknowledged the need to contextualize information about the child's performance and, possibly, to problematize the curricular norms within which any difficulty manifests itself, the Code then relapses into a position in which those norms are effectively taken for granted, and attention is concentrated upon the failings of the individual pupil. The remainder of the Code's guidance is largely concerned with the coordination of the statutory assessment process, and there is little further mention of the possible influence of factors in the school's organization on the pupil's difficulties in learning.

The Code makes reference to the concept of a 'continuum' (6: 22) or 'spectrum' (7: 52) of special educational needs, which was first introduced in the Warnock Report, with the deliberate intention that it should replace the 11 statutory categories of handicap established by the 1944 Education Act, which had previously been used to classify children with disabilities and learning difficulties. The idea of a continuum was usually taken to signify that special educational needs might vary in severity and duration, and often that they might affect pupils of varying levels of intellectual ability. However, the Code also sets out four 'areas of need' into which children's needs are generally expected to fall, namely:

- communication and interaction;
- cognition and learning;
- behaviour, emotional and social development; and
- sensory and/or physical.

There is some tension between the notion of a spectrum of needs and this taxonomy of types of need which are candidates for a statutory statement, that is it suggests that a child's difficulty must fall into one or more of these categories if he/she is to be considered as a potential recipient of the extra resources available through the statementing process.

To summarize, we may say that the Code of Practice is imbued with a contradiction between the formal recognition that difficulties in learning may arise from factors other than the attributes of the individual pupil, including aspects of the school's organization; and the nature of the procedural apparatus of identification and assessment which the body of the Code is concerned to set out. This apparatus is constructed upon a largely individualized model of learning difficulties, in which questions of school organization disappear from the picture once the graduated assessment process has been set in motion. The focus thereafter is upon monitoring and reviewing the performance of the individual pupil within a system of provision whose prevailing norms are taken for granted. Whilst the Code never attempts to set out an explicit theory of learning or pedagogy, one of its main procedural mechanisms, the Individual Education Plan, owes much to an objectives-based model of teaching inspired ultimately by theories of learning derived from behavioural psychology. There is a risk that the system of individualized record-keeping set up by the Code may act as a straitjacket upon more creative, innovative approaches to provision for pupils with difficulties in learning which are based upon the review and development of curriculum and pedagogy across the school as a whole (Clark et al. 1997; Millward and Skidmore 1995, 1998).

Research: continuities and developments within the established paradigms

Turning now to developments in the research literature, we can say first of all that a significant amount of work continues to be published which stands within one or other of the three major traditions which were identified in Chapter 1, that is the psycho-medical, sociological and organizational traditions. The best of this work develops and extends the theoretical frameworks associated with those traditions without, however, overcoming the underlying problem of reductionism: the complex phenomenon of learning difficulties continues to be approached at a single level of analysis. I will briefly illustrate this contention below with reference to each of the established research paradigms, before turning to examine an emerging body of work which adopts a critical perspective towards provision for special educational needs, but avoids a reductionist account of difficulties in learning.

Developments within the psycho-medical paradigm

Considering first the tradition of psycho-medical writing, the 'naughty epidemic' of ADHD (Slee 1996), which was discussed above, continues to spread unabated. Writing about this syndrome in the UK shows many of the same characteristics as the American originals described above, for example the use of a medical vocabulary of 'aetiology and prevalence'; the presumption that the root causes of problematic behaviour can be traced to the child's 'biological make-up'; a proposal for intervention premised on the ethical acceptability of the process of administering medication to pupils to make them better suited to the learning environment; and the call for a 'return to some form of categorical system' for definitions of special educational need (Cooper and Ideus 1995). The jungle of syndromes identified in this tradition continues to burgeon, with new additions being regularly made to the taxonomy of human pathology. The condition of Developmental Coordination Disorder (DCD), or clumsy child syndrome, for instance, has 'recently been accorded formal status by its introduction into the *Diagnostic and Statistical Manual of Mental Disorders*' according to Dussart (Dussart 1994). Dussart reports the construction of a screening checklist to identify children with DCD, using a wide-ranging list of 45 behavioural 'symptoms'. The article is concerned to demonstrate the validity of the instrument by means of the statistical correlation between its results and those of a 'more established instrument', the Test of Motor Impairment. The author puts forward the hypothesis that DCD may be caused by 'bilateral neurological impairment'; but the adoption of this explanation appears to be essentially arbitrary, being unsupported by any evidence reported in the paper, and deriving from a previous hypothesis advanced by other authors in connection with the causes of left-handedness.

These papers may seek to expand the substantive scope of the psycho-medical paradigm, but they break no new theoretical ground, being completely in accord with the characteristic epistemological presuppositions of the paradigm which were identified in Chapter 1. The collection of work found in *Children with Learning Difficulties* (Fawcus 1997), on the other hand, draws on thinking in the fields of genetics and neuroscience to advance a new version of the explanatory model (or theory of causation) associated with the psycho-medical paradigm. The book could be interpreted as an attempt to rehabilitate this tradition in the face of the criticisms levelled at it by many educationists which were noted in the previous chapter. The editor introduces the volume with the claim that psychologists 'have been responsible, more than any other professional group, for bringing about the shift from . . . the medical model of care to a multi-disciplinary approach' (p. xvi). (This assertion runs counter to the view expressed by Tomlinson, for example, that the influence of the profession of educational psychology is one factor behind the expansion of a system of special education founded on a 'humanitarian rhetoric' which conceals the workings of vested interests (Tomlinson 1985).) The new theoretical framework is described by Bowler and Lister Brook, who construct a history of psychological approaches to learning difficulties beginning with psychometric testing (including IQ theory) and culminating in the modern concept of 'behavioural phenotypes' (Bowler and Lister Brook 1997). According to this theory, many kinds of learning difficulty are caused by inherited biological dysfunctions: 'An additional biological cause of mental retardation stems from genetic abnormalities that are inherited by children from their parents' (12). The authors discuss the example of Down's syndrome, then introduce the distinction made in modern genetics between the organism's genotype and phenotype, before going on to note:

> [T]he identification of a genetic basis for Down syndrome led many researchers to explore the possibility that there might be behavioural phenotypes in addition to physical phenotypes that result from specific genetic abnormalities.
>
> (13)

In a second chapter, the same authors offer an account of the work of the clinical psychologist, concentrating particularly on their role in assessing children's behaviour using the 'ABC of functional analysis' (analysing problematic behaviour in terms of antecedents, behaviour and consequences), and in devising therapeutic intervention strategies, notably the application of behaviour modification techniques – 'strategies and methods for reshaping the behaviour of the child under investigation' (Lister Brook and Bowler 1997).

The volume (Fawcus 1997) as a whole is notable for the explicit discussion by some contributors of issues of pedagogy and curriculum in the education of children with learning difficulties (a topic which, as was noted above, has often been lacking in the tradition of psychologically-inspired research). Furthermore, the concept of 'behavioural phenotypes' appears to fill a gap in the theoretical framework of this tradition, which previously lacked a mechanism to account for the incidence of the neurological dysfunctions which were held to be the root cause of many forms of learning difficulty, that is it could not explain why such impairments should occur in the first place. However, a closer inspection reveals that the advance in understanding which the authors claim for the concept of 'behavioural phenotypes' may be less securely anchored than it at first appears. First, it is incorrect to describe Down's syndrome as a 'genetic abnormality inherited by children from their parents'. The most common form of Down's syndrome, standard trisomy-21, which accounts for 95 per cent of cases, is caused by the presence of an extra chromosome, which:

> can come from either the mother or the father, and is present because of a genetic accident when the egg or sperm is made ... or during the initial cell division following conception ... This type of Down's syndrome is always an accident of nature. It can happen to anyone and there is no known reason why it occurs.
>
> (DSA 1995)

Thus, whilst the mechanism which causes Down's syndrome is genetic, it does not occur because of the combination of genes or genotypes which the child inherits from its parents, but as a result of apparently random variations in the reproduction process, and cannot therefore be described as an 'inherited' condition in the sense that (for example) cystic fibrosis is understood to be. Second, whilst most children with Down's syndrome have learning difficulties, as Bowler and Lister Brook themselves note, the degree of learning difficulties associated with the syndrome can vary from severe to non-existent, so it is not clear what contribution an understanding of its genetic basis can make to determining the form of educational provision which is appropriate for an individual child with Down's syndrome.

To generalize from this point, whilst it is clear that conditions exist with a genetic basis which are associated with varying degrees of neurological abnormality, and which may thereby have an effect upon the individual's learning processes, it is far from certain that the concept of 'behavioural phenotypes' can be usefully applied in accounting for most kinds of difficulty in learning; nor is it clear how the correct identification of a genetic basis for a condition can be used to inform or guide the development of pedagogy for any given child or group of children. Finally, it must be asserted that, in contrast to physical characteristics like eye colour, the evidence for the hereditability of complex patterns of human behaviour (such as cognitive activity) remains inconclusive. The widespread existence of 'behavioural phenotypes' which account for a significant proportion of learning difficulties must therefore be treated at present as an unproven conjecture.

Developments within the sociological tradition

Tomlinson and Colquhoun's examination of the 'political economy of special educational needs' represents an impressive contribution to the tradition of sociological research in this area (Tomlinson and Colquhoun 1995). This paper examines the development of a framework of national vocational qualifications (NVQs) in the further education (FE) sector in the 1980s and 1990s in the context of structural changes in the economy, particularly the decline of the youth labour market consequent upon the reduction of unskilled and semi-skilled jobs. It goes on to analyse the impact of this combination upon the economic and social position of young people regarded as having special educational needs. The authors argue that a rhetoric of employability was used to describe the development of vocational courses which 'were in effect behaviourally-oriented programmes of personal self-improvement' (195). They observe that the penalty-driven nature of the funding mechanism for NVQs may result in discrimination against the admission of students with difficulties in learning to FE courses. They also mount a critique of the concept of 'competence', which is central to the assessment apparatus of NVQs and GNVQs (General National Vocational Qualifications), and may dovetail with the development of courses based on a narrow, mechanical curriculum reminiscent of that provided by the early special schools (198). In summary, they predict that the combined effect of these circumstances is likely disproportionately to disadvantage young people regarded as having special educational needs, suggesting that 'special education can itself become a mechanism for legitimating non-employment', and that these policies will result in the production of a 'special (un)employable underclass' (194, 200).

This paper (Tomlinson and Colquhoun 1995) remains avowedly in the tradition of structural sociology, but marks a clear advance over some of the earlier work discussed in Chapter 1. There is a fuller articulation of the relationship between macro-economic developments and the redefinition of the vocational curriculum which began in the mid-1980s. The contradictions between an ideology of learner-centredness and self-improvement, and the reality of structural unemployment, are well-documented and sharply criticized. The research base available at the time, regarding numbers of students and patterns of provision, is reviewed, and its weaknesses are noted. At the same time, however, this piece still carries echoes of the tendency towards hypothetical argument which marred much of the early sociological work, as is evident in the repeated use of phrases such as 'The special are likely to find more difficulty . . .', 'The special may find that . . .' (Tomlinson and Colquhoun 1995: 193, 199); thus, many of the specific criticisms levelled against the emerging policy settlement are based on rationally argued, but essentially speculative projections of its likely effects. The same phrases also suggest that the deterministic outlook of the earlier work persists; young people with special needs are portrayed as an anonymous group of passive victims, whose futures are subject to the workings of impersonal macro-economic forces over which they have no control. It would be unfair to suggest that the authors' outlook was wholly fatalistic, since they briefly allude to examples of alternative policy regimes in other countries, which demonstrate (they suggest) that more inclusive education and employment policies are possible; by implication, therefore, they indicate that central Government in Britain could adopt alternative policies which would redress many of the discriminatory effects of the current 'political economy' of special needs. However, the paper makes no serious attempt to address the concerns of practising educators, having little to say about alternative forms of practice or provision which might be developed by FE practitioners who find themselves working within the constraints of the existing policy settlement. A balanced assessment of the authors' contribution, therefore, must conclude that, whilst their analysis is more thoroughly documented and exhibits greater sophistication than much of the earlier sociological work, some significant 'blind spots' characteristic of the sociological tradition have yet to be overcome.

A powerful and eloquent defence of the importation of sociological theory into research into special education and its relationship with the mainstream has been made by Slee (Slee 1997). Adapting a concept advanced by the liberal postmodernist philosopher, Richard Rorty, Slee criticizes the constraining effect of the 'final local vocabularies' of the discourse of special educational needs upon educational thinking (408). He attacks the appropriation of the language of inclusion by 'assimilationists' for whom inclusion becomes 'a technical problem of resource management' (412). For Slee, by contrast, inclusion remains a fundamentally political project which signifies the need for a radical reconstruction of the system of educational provision; in this enterprise, imported structural and post-structural sociological theory is indispensable, since it provides:

> space ... for alternative policy settlements which may enable teachers and educational administrators to think in different ways about school organisation, curriculum and pedagogy.
>
> (411–12)

Other benefits which result from the importation of sociological theory, according to Slee, include: greater possibilities for changing exclusionary cultures; the problematizing of educators' theories of disability and schooling; and improved clarity in policy analysis (413–16).

This forcefully-argued paper (Slee 1997) epitomizes both the strengths, and the limitations, of a conventional sociological approach to inquiry into issues of inclusion and exclusion in education. Evidence of the existence of structural patterns of discrimination and disadvantage in the education system is rehearsed (for example the well-known over-representation of children from ethnic minorities in referrals for special education, and in exclusions from school). The 'linguistic adjustments' of administrators are ruthlessly exposed, who adopt the vocabulary of inclusion and reverse its meaning, in the interests of perpetuating unreconstructed, exclusionary forms of practice. An equally strongly argued case is made for the likely benefits of a sociologically-inspired retheorizing of current educational practice. Missing from the paper, however, is any real indication of the mechanism whereby such sociological theorizing can be expected to contribute to the transformation of school organization, curriculum and pedagogy *in practice*. On Slee's own evidence, researchers have been elaborating the sociology of special education for the past 15 years, yet in that time, the forces of exclusion from the mainstream have become stronger, not weaker. More specifically, it is surely the responsibility of advocates of inclusive schooling to have something to say to teachers about how, concretely, they might wish to develop their practice in ways which would reduce educational exclusion and enhance the capacity of regular schools to provide for the successful learning of all students. The logic of Slee's position seems to suggest that, if only we import the right quantity of sociological theory into educational research, then pedagogy can safely be left to develop itself. My own view is that, whilst conventional sociological approaches to issues of educational exclusion and inclusion have proved an invaluable source of policy analysis and critique, historically they have had little to say about the process of learning itself, and how this can be facilitated through the development of teaching. Thus, whilst a sociologically-literate perspective may be necessary to the project of inclusion, it is not a sufficient condition for the development of an inclusive pedagogy. The nuanced sociological perspective embodied in the work of Slee and others needs to be supplemented by the incorporation of an adequate psychology of the learning process; I have argued elsewhere that this might take as its point of departure the social constructivist theory of learning, deriving originally from the work of Vygotsky (Skidmore 1996, 1997a, 1997c). If the project of inclusion fails to incorporate such a theory from the outset, then its advocates are likely to find themselves reduced to the endless, and ultimately sterile, recycling of evidence of institutionalized patterns of discrimination.

Developments within the organizational tradition: the idea of the inclusive school

In the previous discussion of the organizational paradigm of research into learning difficulties, I noted that one of the chief theoretical influences on the paradigm was the tradition of school effectiveness research; I further suggested that there was a convergence of interest on the notion of the 'inclusive school'. These two currents are brought together in a study by Rouse and Florian which seeks to define the characteristics of the 'effective inclusive school'(Rouse and Florian 1996). The authors make a comparative, cross-cultural analysis of efforts to restructure mainstream schools to secure greater inclusion in the districts of Utah and Newham. Interviews were conducted in both districts with 'key stakeholders' in the restructuring process (local government officials and school headteachers), in which they were asked to identify the characteristics of effective inclusive schools. The data were analysed by applying Stoll's model of the 12 characteristics of effective schools (Stoll 1991). On the basis of this study, a number of attributes of effective inclusive schools are put forward, including: a common mission; an emphasis on learning; and a climate conducive to learning. In addition, several barriers to the development of effective inclusive schools are discussed (such as differing perceptions by educators of the meaning of inclusion), as is the question of how conditions can be created which facilitate the development of such schools (for example professional development for teachers in the area of collaboration). In conclusion, the authors propose the following definition: 'effective inclusive schools are diverse problem solving organisations with a common mission that emphasises learning for all students.'

Compared with the earliest examples of work within this paradigm, there is a greater formal recognition in Rouse and Florian's paper of factors such as: the significance of school history; the complexity of school development; and the role of the local context. They also note that fundamental questions may arise from the possibility of a tension between the pursuit of excellence (or improved 'effectiveness') in schools and the principle of equity (or greater 'inclusiveness'), an issue which was largely glossed over in the earlier work. Regrettably, however, this observation is not elaborated. As with previous work within this paradigm, a theoretical model developed in the sphere of school effectiveness is adopted uncritically and treated as a touchstone for evaluating efforts to secure increased inclusion, whereas no systematic evidence was presented in the original study as to the inclusive or exclusive character of the schools concerned. One is left with the sense of an opportunity missed. A number of insights are touched upon in passing, which suggest that the authors are sensitive to questions which were beyond the compass of previous work in this paradigm (especially the relevance of broader political issues to the project of inclusion); but these possibilities are largely undeveloped, being subordinated to the authors' determination to use their findings to put forward yet another abstract blueprint of the ideal school.

In their overview of the themes emerging from the literature on inclusive schooling, Sebba and Ainscow (Sebba and Ainscow 1996) identify four broad issues: defining inclusion; school organization and development; classroom processes; and teacher development. After discussing the criteria which should be taken into account in defining the term, they arrive at the following formulation:

> Inclusion describes the process by which a school attempts to respond to all pupils as individuals by reconsidering its curricular organisation and provision. Through this process, the school builds its capacity to accept all pupils from the local community who wish to attend and, in so doing, reduces the need to exclude pupils.
>
> (9)

They contend that inclusion in this sense is closely connected with school effectiveness, and argue that inclusive schools take on the features of the 'learning organization'. Noting that cultural change in schools often leads to a period of organizational 'turbulence', they suggest that the literature on school development provides examples of arrangements which may help to manage this phenomenon. They go on to review research on the intra-class grouping arrangements and teaching styles which are best adapted to inclusive settings. Finally, the importance of teacher development in increasing educational inclusion is affirmed, and a number of school- and classroom-based strategies for supporting that development are instanced, such as workshops on active learning approaches and partnerships which encourage dialogue between teachers.

As in earlier work in the organizational tradition, in this article the process of inclusion is explicitly identified with overall school development and school effectiveness; but in several respects the authors go beyond the limitations of earlier work in this tradition. For example, the case for inclusion is no longer argued on purely philosophical grounds; rather, the authors draw attention to the research base which substantiates the beneficial effects of inclusion on the academic and social outcomes of schooling. The prospect of a new conception of pedagogical development, transcending the inculcation of narrow technical competences, is also foreshadowed in the recognition of the importance of improvisation in the classroom, and the encouragement of structured dialogues between teachers as a means of improving their own practice. Against this, other weaknesses associated with the tradition remain. First, to equate inclusion with school effectiveness is to ignore the tension between the pressure upon schools to maximize pupil performance in public examinations, and the aspiration to accept and provide for the full diversity of pupils in the local community, including those who may perform poorly in conventional academic tasks. Second, little cognisance is taken of the impact of national education policy on developments within the school. The authors, for example, argue in favour of mixed ability classes, and against systems of setting, banding and streaming (Sebba and Ainscow 1996: 12–13). The advantages of mixed groupings are clearly articulated, but in making policy decisions on this question, it is scarcely possible for schools to ignore the tone of the national policy debate; throughout the 1990s, Government statements indicated official support for increased use of banding and other forms of ability grouping. Finally, the conception of school change embodied in the metaphor of 'turbulence' implicitly presupposes a state of organizational equilibrium as the norm. Yet if (as the authors themselves argue) inclusion is to be seen as a process, rather than a fixed state, then it is a fallacy to conceptualize its inception as a storm to be weathered, before the harbour of tranquillity is regained. The attempt to 'respond to all pupils as individuals' is likely to require schools continuously to scrutinize and modify their organizational structures and practices; hence, the process of change will be open-ended.

Critical perspectives: views of the processes of inclusion and exclusion in schooling

In the foregoing sections I have documented the contention that a significant amount of work continues to be published which, whilst it may extend the major research traditions at their margins, does not mark a fundamental departure from their characteristic modes of explanation. It would be a mistake, however, to suppose that research into special needs education in the mid-1990s was confined to reworkings of one or other of the established paradigms. This section will review a number of works which adopt a critical perspective towards existing educational practice, but which avoid the reductionist explanations of earlier approaches, and thereby enlarge the theoretical apparatus at our disposal in this field.

A major contribution to thinking about discipline policy in education is made by Slee in *Changing Theories and Practices of Discipline* (Slee 1995). Though the purview of this book is not restricted to 'special needs' in the narrow sense of academic difficulties in learning, Slee's work has a clear bearing on debate about pupils 'at risk of failing' in the educational system. The book's central aim is to provide the groundwork for an 'educational theory of discipline' (17). Slee distinguishes between reductionist accounts of discipline as control and theorizing which reconceptualizes discipline in ways consistent with the educational aims of schooling. Tracing the history of the use of corporal punishment in Australian schools, he demonstrates that its abolition did not lead to a reconsideration of relationships of authority, but to a search for new forms of control (166). In this context, he critiques the growing influence of educational psychology and the associated 'behaviour industry' with its tendency to problematize the individual student in isolation from considerations of school context. In contrast, Slee seeks to broaden the focus of debate, arguing that 'the antecedents of disruption are not simply bound to individual pathologies' (167), and drawing on a sociological framework to illustrate the differential impact of discipline policies in relation to gender, class and ethnicity. Examining the history of policy developments in various Australian states with respect to school discipline, he points out that the predominance of the 'control paradigm' has led to the formulation of policies which fail to consider the role of school organization, curriculum and pedagogy in developing a response to disruption. He goes on to present evidence of alternative school improvement initiatives in three schools which were successful in reducing student disaffection and improving outcomes. A major feature in each case was the direct participation of students and the local community in decisions about changing the school's policy and practice. Slee comments:

> [The school's] interventions to effect improved outcomes for . . . students were not constructed according to changing student pathologies, but to an ascertainment of the school's pathology and a process of intense treatment of the school organization, culture, curriculum and teaching and learning strategies.
>
> (168)

The study concludes with a set of recommendations which provide an alternative theoretical framework which could be used to guide future research and policy development in the area of school discipline. Major recommendations include:

- that discipline should be reconceptualized as an educational issue as distinct from a question of managerial control;
- that the complexity of the causes of disruptive behaviour in schools should be recognized, and that responses to it should not be confined to medical interventions;
- that the contribution of curriculum, pedagogy and school organization to the production and reduction of disaffection should be recognized in education policy; and
- that those affected by policies (in this case, particularly school students) should participate in all phases of the policy-making process.

(170–9)

It will be clear from the foregoing account that Slee's contribution shares with earlier sociological work an insistence on the need to locate educational problems in a broader societal context, which includes for example consideration of the effects of youth unemployment on the incidence of disaffection in schools (a point also made by Tomlinson in her sociological analysis of changes in special education policy (Tomlinson 1985)). Like this previous work, Slee is also concerned to demonstrate the connection between policies formulated in the education sphere and structural patterns of social advantage and disadvantage such as gender, class and ethnicity. Slee's analysis, however, marks a theoretical advance over some previous sociologically-inspired studies, in that it does not suggest that institutional conditions in schools can be 'read off' in any transparent way from macro-social conditions (avoiding the problem of reductionism). It is informed by evidence of the effects of concrete initiatives in schools aimed at reducing student disaffection, and thus also avoids the charge of determinism; the vignettes of particular schools show clearly that institutional reform initiatives which are informed by an educational conception of discipline (as opposed to a 'control' perspective) can bring positive benefits in improving students' achievements, as well as being more consistent with the principle of equity. Whilst building on the strengths of the sociological tradition of inquiry into education, Slee's conceptually sophisticated approach avoids the twin weaknesses of reductionism and determinism which marred some earlier work in this tradition, and provides a useful model of how an important issue of education policy can be approached from a perspective which is informed both by relevant critical theory and by evidence of the concrete possibility of alternative forms of practice.

Another significant contribution to the literature which adopts a critical perspective on special needs education is found in *Bad-Mouthing: The Language of Special Needs* (Corbett 1996). Like Slee, Corbett stresses the need to situate the question of education policy in relation to pupils with disabilities in a broader frame of reference. Several of the texts presented for discussion in the book are drawn from the disability arts movement, for instance, as part of a deliberate strategy to broaden debate in the field by shifting it away from a narrow preoccupation with specific aspects of the formal schooling system. The author also continues the concern associated with the sociological tradition to 'deconstruct' or make problematic the concepts and terminology which are conventionally employed to discuss provision for pupils with difficulties in learning. Thus, she begins by analysing the 'voice of enlightened modernity' articulated in the Warnock Report, which introduced the currently dominant establishment discourse revolving around the central concept of 'special educational needs' itself. She proceeds to identify four distinct 'discourses' which are currently constitutive of the language of special needs, that is: psychology; sociology; philosophy; and politics (18–25). She then argues the need to move from the current position, defined by a stratified hierarchy of 'dominant' discourses, to one in which a series of alternative, parallel discourses will co-exist side by side, a position in which 'the diversity of voices are of equal status' (34). This entails the need for a shift in attitudes towards 'celebrating difference' instead of employing a vocabulary of negative, stigma-laden labels. As an indication of the state of affairs which this reconstructive project might bring about, Corbett invokes an analogy with music, notably the spontaneous improvisation of jazz (74 ff.), a genre in which a new harmony is created out of highly diverse individual contributions. She identifies three particular 'tunes' or discourses which might forge a new language of disability pride (75): the social model of disability; the civil rights movements of disabled people and others; and the political treatment of personal experience in disability arts. Important attributes which need to be fostered if this new language is to be brought into being include the skill of 'active listening' to the words of others whose lifeworlds may be different from our own, and a sense of humility before the diversity of human experience.

As is the case with Slee's work, Corbett's book rejects the determinism which sometimes characterized early critical accounts of special education; indeed, it is very much alive to the political self-activity of disabled people as one of the forces which is challenging existing thinking and reshaping practice in this area. Her detailed reading of a range of texts in all their specificity is also far removed from the tendency towards abstraction which was sometimes present in this earlier work. The tone of this book expresses the author's active commitment to combating linguistic practices which discriminate against those with disabilities and difficulties in learning, a commitment which is at the same time combined with a reflexive self-awareness of the difficulties and complexities of this struggle.

Susan Hart's valuable book, *Beyond Special Needs*, furnishes an example of another work which is broadly transformative in intent, though this time the focus is directly upon the minutiae of intersubjective interaction between teacher and pupil (Hart 1996). The book derives from a study conducted by the author over the course of a school year into the effects of a 'process' approach to the teaching of literacy, by close examination of the writing development of two pupils nearing the end of their primary schooling. The research design employed, which is a qualitative, case study approach, quasi-ethnographic in character, results in a nuanced, individualized portrait of the two pupils' development, which provides a welcome contrast to the exclusive reliance placed by many cohort studies upon crude quantitative outcome measures, which are inherently incapable of offering any insight into the *process* of learning.

Hart shows how one pupil ('Annette') unexpectedly responded to the writing workshop environment by evolving standard, routinized structures for producing extended prose, a development for which she usefully coins the term 'repertoire-writing'. In the case of a second pupil ('Adrian'), the workshop environment provided the motivation to experiment with new textual structures in his writing; but the author shows how the subjective intentions which drove him were quite different from the intentions which his teachers had in mind in devising the workshop setting. In reflecting on these case studies, the author reminds us that pupils' cognitive development cannot be understood as a linear upward progression; by way of contrast, she puts forward a rationalist view of learning framed in terms of intrinsic growth.

The centrepiece of Hart's book is its presentation of a conceptual framework which the author terms 'Innovative Thinking'. This consists of five 'interpretative moves' which the author suggests as guidelines for teachers' thinking about concerns over children's learning. The five moves are:

- *making connections* between contextual features of the classroom environment and children's learning;
- *contradicting* the widely-held normative assumptions which lead to a child's response being perceived as problematic;
- *taking the child's eye view*, or seeking to understand the meaning which an activity may hold for the pupil;
- *examining the impact of our own feelings* on the interpretation we make of a situation; and
- *suspending judgement* where we need to acquire further conceptual resources in arriving at an evaluation of a child's progress.

(8)

The narratives constructed to account for the cognitive development of the two pupils on whom the study was centred illustrate in practice how this framework can be used to generate an open-ended, self-reflexive understanding of children's learning, which reasons outwards from a close study of particular individuals to questions which are of general pedagogical significance.

The book is informed by the author's substantial and varied teaching experience, which leads to a subtle, textured analysis, according due recognition to the inherent complexities of the teacher's task, providing a welcome relief from the frequent attempts which have been made in recent years to reduce pedagogical expertise to a checklist of technical competencies. The author places a refreshing emphasis upon the dynamic, interactive nature of learning and teaching, reminding us of the need to recognize the active part played by all pupils in shaping their own learning, which is mediated through the agendas which they bring to bear on classroom activities, which may be quite different from the agendas of their teachers. The book also conveys a genuine, powerful desire to assist in the creation of mainstream schools which are more learner-oriented: it is clear that the author is committed to the principle of a much more inclusive system of schooling.

As Hart acknowledges (128), the most important theoretical influence upon this work is the concept of the reflective practitioner initiated by the work of Schön (1983); the specific transformation of Schön's work in the field of education which produced the tradition of research into 'teacher thinking' may also be detected as a subsidiary influence. Within the context of a recognition of Hart's positive achievements, two issues may be noted which place limitations on the applicability of the Innovative Thinking framework as it is formulated in Hart's book (1996). First, the framework operates with an implicitly individualistic model of teaching, predicated on the image of the lone teacher striving to improve her own classroom practice in isolation. This stance may underestimate the importance of dialogue with others (in addition to the internal dialogue of self-reflection) in challenging and developing teachers' thinking and practice. A second, connected issue is that the framework neglects the micropolitical dimension of schoolteaching. Whilst Hart argues that the framework can be applied to thinking about school-wide development initiatives, as well as to the learning of individual pupils in the classroom, this appears to be more a matter of speculation than a conclusion which is firmly rooted in the research reported, which was not designed to gather direct evidence of school-wide processes in a systematic way. Notwithstanding these criticisms, Hart's book forms a significant contribution to the literature, which offers a framework which will be found to be of practical use by teachers struggling to enhance children's learning, without denying the inherent complexity and uncertainty of the teacher's task.

Painting on a broader canvas, the authors of *New Directions in Special Needs: Innovations in Mainstream Schools* (Clark et al. 1997) situate the current state of provision for special needs in mainstream schools in the historical perspective of the period from the end of World War 2 to the present day. They also draw on the findings of a number of research projects to offer an empirically-grounded portrait of innovative approaches to special needs provision in the 1990s, and the problems and contradictions which beset them in practice. They begin by positing a 'fundamental dilemma' in the aim of establishing a *universal* system of provision for a population which is *non-homogeneous*. They then analyse the historical context in terms of a series of partial, incomplete attempts to resolve this dilemma, setting out the following periodization scheme:

- the pattern of *segregation and selection* both between and within schools established by the 1944 Education Act;
- the growth of *special classes* in mainstream schools during the 1960s;
- the establishment of *remedial provision* through the 1960s and 1970s;
- the development of 'complex *mixed economies* of special or quasi-special education' alongside mainstream provision which characterized many comprehensive schools in the late 1970s; and
- the emergence of the *whole school approach*, which sought to educate children with special needs alongside their peers in mainstream classrooms, and which acquired 'the status of an orthodoxy in thinking about special needs education' in the 1980s.

(3–10)

A more detailed examination of the whole school approach follows. This detects evidence of three 'patterns of failure' in the history of the approach, that is the resistance which it encountered from the mainstream; the replication of features of special education; and ambiguities and contradictions internal to the approach itself. The whole school approach is portrayed as the latest in a series of attempts to merge mainstream and special education, as opposed to setting out to transform the mainstream itself. The authors conclude that, whilst the balance sheet may not show outright failure, it does tell a tale in which the values underpinning the approach were only incompletely realized in practice.

The book then goes on to summarize the findings of several research studies conducted at the beginning of the 1990s into 'innovatory' special needs practice in mainstream schools. An 'emerging model' is identified (41), at the heart of which lies the project of developing an inclusive and differentiated pedagogy. This is buttressed by the application of strategies for the management of institutional change; flexible resource management; staff development; and the facilitation of collaborative working. The 'innovatory' quality of the model is seen to inhere less in the surface features of provision than in the underlying coherence of its aims and strategies. The book then contextualizes this model by exploring the emergence of the policy of integration (stimulated in England and Wales in the period following the 1981 Education Act). The concept of integration is seen as suffering from inherent limitations (84 ff.) because it is circumscribed by clauses of conditionality, embodied in the famous formula of the Warnock Report, which was carried over into legislation, that an integrated placement was to be preferred subject to: its capacity to meet the child's special needs; its compatibility with the effective education of the child's mainstream peers; and the efficient use of resources (86). A second limitation inherent in the concept of integration was that the overriding consideration was to be the delivery of special educational provision. As in the case of the whole school approach, the integration movement is seen as an attempt to bring the special and mainstream sectors closer together without effecting a radical reconstruction of the mainstream, whose fundamental conditions of existence are taken for granted.

The authors then examine the inclusive schools movement, which has been put forward as a radical alternative to integration. The distinctive feature of this philosophy is that it rests upon a notion of inalienable human rights, which brook no clauses of conditionality. The authors suggest that two unresolved dilemmas may still face the movement for inclusion as it is presently constituted: the dilemma between the aims of education for *all* and education for *each*; and the dilemma between the provision of *common* educational experiences and the provision of *appropriate* experiences (100).

Finally, in attempting to draw out the theoretical lessons of this analysis, the authors propose a two-part model of change in special needs education (173 ff.). First, they situate provision for special needs at the school level in a matrix of internal and external constraints and possibilities which may affect the development of that provision (for example demographic issues, government policy in education and other spheres of social policy, the micro-political climate of the school; 174). Then, they propose that analyses of systemic change in special needs education must take account of the following generic factors: prevailing social and educational values; the social and political context; available educational technologies; and dilemmas intrinsic to the mass provision of education, and the specific resolutions which are currently proposed in response to those dilemmas (176).

One merit of this text is that it avoids reductionist explanations of the development of special needs education whether of the sociological, psychological or organizational variety, attempting instead to convey a sense of the complexity of the flux of historical development as it pertains to education policy and patterns of provision. In a field marked by the assertion of a priori value positions, it also benefits by drawing on a substantial evidential base of empirically-grounded inquiries into the contemporary configuration of provision in schools, and into developments in patterns of provision at the regional level. Its analysis does not construct a linear narrative (whether of progress or decline), but is alert to the convolutions and contingencies of the historical process, and is open-eyed in confronting the partial, incomplete nature of attempts to develop a unified, non-categorical system of provision, penetrating below the level of rhetoric to assess the impact of policy on provision in schools.

A more extended historical perspective on the development of patterns of special educational provision can be found in the work of Copeland (I. Copeland 1995, 1996, 1997), who has shown that the roots of many contemporary debates can be traced back to decisions taken at the very origins of the modern education system. He begins by deploying theoretical constructs adapted from Bourdieu (the theory of cultural capital) and Weber (the concept of status groups) to interpret the proceedings of the Royal Commission on the Blind, the Deaf and Dumb &c. (1886–8), chaired by Lord Egerton (Copeland 1995). The Commission's original terms of reference were extended to incorporate 'such other cases as from special circumstances would seem to require exceptional methods of education', but its report paid much less attention to this class of pupils (which it interpreted as referring to the 'educable class of imbeciles'), despite the fact that they far outnumbered the blind and the deaf. From the outset it accepted that it was dealing with cases which lay beyond the scope of elementary schools, setting up a predisposition in favour of segregated provision, which arguably 'put a fence around the potential for social interaction and a ceiling upon expectations of development' (Copeland 1995: 185).

Copeland's account of the Egerton Commission's deliberations upon the education of 'idiots and imbeciles' revolves around the contrast between the evidence presented by two of its major witnesses, G. Shuttleworth and F. Warner. Shuttleworth offered a definition of idiocy and imbecility in terms of a relative degradation of intellect; argued for a clinical aetiology; and advocated the establishment of a separate system of residential special schools, with a restricted 'practical' curriculum of vocational activities and physical exercise. Warner's evidence was concerned rather with 'feeble-minded' children; he offered an interactionist aetiology framed in terms of the combined effects of social and personal circumstances, and the inadequate conditions prevailing in the ordinary curriculum of elementary schools. He proposed the establishment of small special classes within elementary schools, and had devised a system of assessment whereby teachers themselves (without the assistance of medical officers) could identify children for admission to these classes. As Copeland points out, whilst Warner's proposals would have entailed a systemic reform of elementary schools, Shuttleworth's insulated the mainstream system from the need for change. The Commission's report endorsed Shuttleworth's ideas, which thus constituted the 'first economy of learning disability' (1995), on which much later practice was founded.

Copeland develops his interpretation of the early history of special education in England by applying the Foucauldian concept of normalization (Copeland 1996), which 'involves the five processes of comparison, differentiation, hierarchisation, homogenisation and exclusion' (382). He shows the operation of each of these processes in the deliberations of the Egerton Commission and the subsequent Departmental Committee on Defective and Epileptic Children (1897–8). This Committee was strongly influenced by the policies of the School Board for London, which was already operating a system of segregated special schools, to which pupils were admitted on basis of an examination supervised by a medical officer. The London Board was attached to the principle of classifying pupils to the maximum extent possible (387). Its system is contrasted with the alternative model of the Leicester Board (which was also described in evidence to the Committee), which operated a system of special classes *within* elementary schools, to which pupils were admitted on the basis of an educational assessment. Leicester's School Inspector expressed a commitment to the placement of all pupils in ordinary schools wherever possible (389). The Committee endorsed the principle, expounded by Shuttleworth, of a hierarchical classification of mental deficiency. This principle then passed into legislation in the Elementary Education (Defective and Epileptic Children) Act 1899, which adopted the same definition of defective children in terms of a gradation of mental deficiency. Copeland concludes that the policies of the Leicester Board and the School Board for London represented 'contrasting forms of rationality' (392); the Leicester Board applied an educational norm in determining the organization of provision, whereas the organizing principle applied by the School Board for London was a classification of intellect according to the precepts of medical science. The practices of the London Board produced a 'powerful blueprint for a subsystem' which was widely adopted, despite the existence of an alternative model from the outset.

The ramifications of this analysis for an understanding of the subsequent development of special education in England are made explicit in a later paper (I. Copeland 1997), where Copeland exploits the Foucauldian concept of 'genealogy', understood as the writing of the history of the present. Returning to the Egerton Commission's Report, he suggests that it carried two major consequences for pupils with learning difficulties: first, they became 'part of the domain supervised by the medical profession'; and second, the quest for an educational solution was closed off. Reviewing the evidence presented on behalf of the Leicester School Board to the Departmental Committee on Defective and Epileptic Children, he suggests that it represented the 'first practical scheme for inclusive education'. The model of provision developed by the School Board for London, on the other hand, represented the 'blueprint for segregated special schools'. Copeland then sketches a series of subsequent milestones in the development of special education policy during the twentieth century, before concluding that the contemporary legacy of the London Board can be seen, concretely, in the existence of a national network of segregated special schools; practically, in the set of procedures which are routinely undertaken in making special educational provision; and, ideologically, in the body of ideas and theories which support this nexus of practice.

Copeland's contribution in this sequence of papers consists above all in his demonstration of the radical historicity of the contemporary practice of special education. His analysis of early Government inquiries into this question excavates the forgotten foundations on which current policies have been overlaid. Like the other writing reviewed in this section, his work eschews any suggestion of historical determinism, illuminating the highly contingent nature of policy decisions taken at the turn of the last century, which have nevertheless cast a long shadow over the development of provision up to the present day. As, today, the debate over the inclusion of pupils with difficulties in learning revives with renewed vigour, it is pertinent for us to be reminded that the system of educational provision which surrounds us is not an inevitable product of the laws of nature, but the outcome of a specific process of historical development. In particular, it is important to recognize that the segregated system of special education which became the norm was not the only available option, and that, at the very beginnings of the modern education system, an alternative, more inclusive model of provision was extant in the policies of the Leicester Board.

Julie Allan's work also makes a strong case for the applicability of a Foucauldian theoretical framework to the field; her focus is directly upon contemporary practice in special needs education. She suggests that Foucault's work offers a 'box of tools' for analysing the effects of the policy of mainstreaming, especially upon the experiences of the children involved (Allan 1996). She notes the distinction between the methodology of 'archaeology' (a historiography of truth claims) developed in Foucault's earlier work, and his later 'genealogical' approach, which is preoccupied with the operation of power in institutional settings. Following Foucault, she sets out a number of 'techniques of surveillance' which construct individuals as subjects and objects of 'knowledge/power', that peculiarly impersonal and disembodied oppressive force which haunts Foucault's writings. She distinguishes three such techniques, offering examples of how they might be said to operate in special educational practice.

- *hierarchical observation* – evident in the special scrutiny to which children with special educational needs are subject;
- *normalizing judgements* – present, for example, in the determination of the cut-off point for issuing a Record of Needs; and,
- *examination* – most evident in the multi-disciplinary assessment procedure.

Elaborating on this analysis, Allan notes how:

> Following the assessment, the child with special educational needs is marked out for perpetual surveillance throughout the remainder of his or her school career and beyond.
>
> (224)

She goes on to identify a set of analytical 'tools' devised by Foucault which may be of service in unmasking the operation of 'knowledge/power' upon children with special educational needs, selecting for particular attention the techniques of 'reversal' (inverting the conclusions of official discourses as a means of rethinking the phenomenon in question) and 'discontinuity' (the search for gaps and disjunctures in these discourses). She compares the Foucauldian perspective to other approaches to theorizing special educational needs, namely: the essentialist perspective of the within-child deficit model; the social constructionist perspective, notable for its critique of labelling and categorization; and the social creationist perspective, which locates the problem of discrimination against the disabled in the institutionalized practices of society. Arguing that 'It may not be possible or appropriate to establish a single theory of special educational needs' (227), she suggests that a post-modernist perspective derived from Foucault allows for the real 'plurality of voices' which characterizes the field in a way which other theoretical approaches fail to take account of. She concludes her paper by listing a number of findings from her analysis of the experiences of children with special educational needs from a Foucauldian perspective, most notably that 'mainstream pupils operated a mini regime of governmentality'.

Allan extends this analysis in a paper delivered at the international seminar on 'Theoretical Perspectives on Special Education', held in Ålesund, Norway, in May 1997 (Allan 1997; Skidmore 1997b). In this presentation, Allan criticizes the 'technical and empiricist bases of knowledge production and the "methodological individualism" of researchers' in the field of special education (1); she also takes to task the perspective of 'enlightened modernity' which constructs the world through such simplistic binarisms as the opposition between integrated and segregated placements (neglecting to examine the quality of the educational experiences which take place in those settings). Rehearsing the case for adopting a Foucauldian perspective, she reports and discusses a sample of pupils' accounts of their experiences of inclusion, drawing on the words of both mainstream pupils and pupils with special educational needs. She identifies four features of the 'regime of governmentality' practised by mainstream pupils:

- the exercise of *pastoral power*, including the attempt to 'erase difference' involved in the claim that pupils with difficulties should be 'treated like us';
- the adoption of *pedagogic strategies*, in which mainstream pupils assume the role of agents of the academic and social development of pupils with special needs;
- the strategy of *allowing transgressions*, or permitting breaches of the normal rules concerning intimacy between pupils; and
- *legitimizing exclusion*, the finding that mainstream pupils' conduct could be highly punitive, and might extend to the verbal bullying of pupils with learning difficulties.

But Allan is not only concerned with the experiences of pupils who have always been in the mainstream; she also draws on the accounts of pupils with special educational needs to illustrate their 'practices of the self' (1997: 9). She shows how pupils with disabilities (for example visual impairment) challenge and resist the disabled identities which are constructed for them, notably by teachers and other professionals. This allows them actively to shape their own identities, albeit at the risk of conflict with those in authority over them. Finally, Allan draws out the implications of a Foucauldian analysis for the project of building 'schools for all'. Whilst rejecting a rose-tinted view of pupils' behaviour, she affirms the possibility of harnessing and reinforcing the positive aspects of the 'regime of governmentality' operated by mainstream pupils, so that: 'Schools for all . . . are schools which are created by, rather than for, all pupils' (14).

One of the most fruitful insights of Allan's work is the critical light which it throws upon the whole apparatus of identification and assessment which surrounds provision for pupils with special educational needs. Previous analyses had indicated the 'gatekeeping' role played by educational psychologists in the process of statutory assessment (for example Dessent (1987), who describes the educational psychologist as the 'definer of resourceworthiness'). Allan's analysis suggests that the assessment procedure carries a still more profound significance, as a species of 'examination' in the Foucauldian sense of a ritual determination of difference, an ascertainment of *ab*normality (or distance from the norm) which thereby defines what it is to be educationally 'normal'. Whilst acknowledging the chief criticism which is justly levelled at Foucault, that he consistently refused to spell out what should be done in response to the depredations wrought by the operation of 'power/knowledge', Allan seems to eschew such fatalism in her own work; she shares with many of the studies previously discussed an interest in the possibility of transformative action which will lead to the creation of more inclusive forms of school provision.

In an insightful contribution to a special issue of the *Cambridge Journal of Education* on international developments in inclusive schooling (vol. 26, no. 1), Tony Booth also offers a critical perspective, informed by empirical evidence, upon contemporary processes of inclusion and exclusion in schools, in this case concentrating on the current situation in England (Booth 1996). With collaborating colleagues at the Open University, Booth has played a leading role in developing thinking in this field, and has been an active advocate for integration, understood as the development of comprehensive community education. Like Allan, Booth in this paper makes use of evidence from observational studies focusing on the experiences of individual pupils to substantiate his analysis, though seeking more explicitly to locate these experiences within the context of educational policy and legislation. Booth takes as his point of departure 'the assumption of diversity in common groups' (1996: 88). Arguing against the idea that inclusion can be thought of as an ideal state, which can be studied through cataloguing examples of 'good practice', he suggests instead that it should be thought of as a set of processes, proposing the following definition:

> [Inclusion] comprises two linked processes: it is the process of increasing the *participation* of students in the cultures and curricula of mainstream schools and communities; it is the process of reducing the *exclusion* of students from mainstream cultures and curricula.
>
> (91; emphases added)

After reviewing developments in legislation and case law in England and Wales, he goes on to show how research can illuminate these twin processes of participation and exclusion by investigating how schools respond to student differences, drawing on two studies to illustrate this argument. First, he describes a study of the inclusion of students with Down's syndrome in secondary schools in eight local authorities, which reveals that the proportion of students in mainstream schools varied very widely between authorities, concluding that such discrepancies 'can only be the result of local policies, rather than the characteristics of students' (93). This picture is augmented by an observational study of the different opportunities for participation extended to two students with Down's syndrome in the same school, revealing major anomalies, which Booth concludes are best explained by the dual support systems operating in the school, rather than by any significant difference in student characteristics. He also reports preliminary reflections arising from a second observational study of participation in a mainstream secondary school, in which a number of students were shadowed through a range of curricular activities. The study documents variations in the possibilities for participation available to a number of individual students in different areas of the curriculum, and significant variations in the degree of exclusion and participation experienced by one student within a single lesson. Drawing on evidence of the beliefs and attitudes of teachers, Booth indicates some of the contradictory pressures at work in the culture and curriculum of the school, which tend to reinforce exclusionary or inclusive forms of practice. He concludes by arguing for a broad understanding of the term inclusion, which should not be confined to a narrow preoccupation with disabled students or those identified as having 'special needs'.

An important achievement of Booth's paper is to demonstrate how the gap between the theoretical analysis of policy and empirically-based investigations of practice in schools can be bridged. Booth explores how concepts used in legislation exercise a constraining effect upon the development of educational thinking, and ultimately contribute to the exclusionary pressures at work on the careers of individual pupils. This applies particularly to the concept of 'special educational need'; like Corbett (1996), Booth advocates that the use of this term should be abandoned. But whereas earlier sociological work was often content to discuss the effects of policy in purely abstract terms, Booth is here concerned to illustrate his argument through a presentation of empirical evidence, both statistical and qualitative in kind. Life in school is set within the broader context defined by education policy, but is at the same time brought alive in all its concrete particularity, through the depiction of specific occurrences of participation and exclusion experienced by individual students. It is also clear that many of the instances of exclusion experienced by pupils are not the automatic or inevitable consequence of national policy. If students within the same school can have different experiences of participation in and exclusion from the curriculum in ways which are not attributable to their individual characteristics; and if the same student can participate successfully in some areas of school life (including areas of the mainstream curriculum) whilst repeatedly experiencing exclusion from others; then it suggests that action can be taken at the school and classroom level, *as well as* at the level of national policy, to increase the participation and reduce the exclusion of students from mainstream cultures and curricula. This perspective rejects the abstract determinism of some sociological work in favour of a view of educational inclusion as a process which may be constrained by forces operating beyond the school, but can be enhanced or held back in ways which make a real difference to individual pupils by the activities and dispositions of practitioners in schools. The combination of sophisticated theoretical analysis and detailed evidence of the particulars of classroom experiences offers a powerful model for future research in this field.

A plethora of books have been published in recent years concerning comparative policy on the education of disabled students in different national contexts (Booth and Ainscow 1998; Vitello and Mithaug 1998; Armstrong et al. 2000). In *Education and children with special needs: From segregation to inclusion* (Hegarty and Alur 2002), the contributors set out to describe current policy and provision in India, and to compare and contrast this with policy regimes in a number of other countries. The book takes the form of an edited collection of 22 chapters, divided into two parts: national perspectives on policy in India, and international perspectives on policy and practice. The book arises out of a series of seminars held in different locations in India in 1997, sponsored by the Indian Government. Mithu Alur has a long history of campaigning and involvement in the development of services for disabled children and is founder chairperson of the Spastics Society of India. Seamus Hegarty has published extensively on special needs education and is the Director of the National Foundation of Educational Research in England and Wales.

The first part of the book provides a series of accounts of the main features of national and local policy on the education of disabled people in India. These are helpful in explaining the background and current state of provision for those previously unfamiliar with the national context. Mithu Alur provides a historical account of the development of policy affecting the education of disabled people in India since Independence (Alur 2002b). She documents how the transfer of responsibility from the Ministry of Education in 1964 to the Ministry of Welfare led to a paternalistic policy of grant-assisted, piecemeal provision by voluntary organizations. National Government effectively abdicated its responsibility for educating disabled children. She mounts a severe critique of the prevailing policy vacuum, characterized by a lack of political will, and a contradiction between policy proclamations favouring integration on the one hand, and a continued practice of neglect on the other, in which 90 per cent of disabled people receive no service provision from the state. P. R. Dasgupta, who was secretary of the Ministry of Education and Human Resource Development at the time of the seminars, describes Government initiatives on the education of disabled children in the previous two decades (Dasgupta 2002). He acknowledges that, out of an estimated 10–15 million disabled children in the country, only about 60,000 children are enrolled in special schools, and a further 50,000 disabled children are integrated in mainstream schools, confirming the general picture of exclusion and neglect painted by Alur. Ruma Banerjee describes a community-based rehabilitation programme in the rural district of Bangalore organized by a voluntary organization which she co-directs (Banerjee 2002). The project demonstrates the importance of organized action at the village level, while at the same time highlighting the fundamental issue of poverty which shapes the lives of families of agricultural workers: many parents are necessarily so preoccupied with labouring to sustain their livelihood that they have little time or energy to give to meeting the educational needs of a disabled child. Usha Singh, a school principal from Jaipur, offers a series of case studies of integration of children with various disabilities in mainstream settings (Singh 2002). Their successes were not achieved without struggle, on their own part and that of their teachers, but what comes through is the determination of many of these children to participate fully with their peers in the social and academic life of the school, on their own terms. Other chapters deal with projects to provide education for disabled children in Calcutta, and teacher training initiatives funded by UNESCO.

The second part of the book contains contributions from commentators from economically developed countries, including the UK, Sweden, Denmark and Israel, which go some way towards raising the complex issues of international/cross-cultural development work in this area. Mark Vaughan, co-director of the Centre for Studies in Inclusive Education in England, reviews the shift towards increased support for inclusion in international policy pronouncements such as the UN Convention on the Rights of the Child and the UNESCO Salamanca Statement (Vaughan 2002). He also mentions examples of district-level inclusion initiatives from North America and England. He argues powerfully for inclusion as an issue of human rights, pointing out the discrimination inherent in segregating disabled students. Seamus Hegarty discusses the issues at the level of the education system and national policy which need to be confronted in efforts to develop a system of comprehensive education (Hegarty 2002). He identifies a possible 'legislative gap' between the Indian Constitution's commitment to provision for disabled people and the apparent absence of detailed policies on rights and responsibilities in the education service, for example on parents' rights to be involved in decisions regarding the education of their children. Malini Chib, an advocate of equal opportunities for disabled people, provides a powerful account of her experience of exclusion in education, both in a special school, where geographical separation meant there was no opportunity for her to mix with her peers after school hours, and in a regular school, where she suffered from social isolation and a lack of meaningful friendships (Chib 2002). In spite of these difficulties, she later attained success in a higher education course where staff made accommodations to her needs, while expecting as much from her in terms of learning as from non-disabled students.

Hegarty and Alur (2002) present factual information about Indian policy on the education of disabled people which is not easily available elsewhere, and make a welcome addition to the literature for this reason. Perhaps the most valuable contribution it makes is to document the scale of social exclusion which continues to be experienced by disabled people in the country, a legacy in part of the history of British colonialism, which encouraged the development of a higher education system capable of producing a local elite to administer the dominion, but gave no serious attention to mass elementary education. It is also an indictment of the complacency and muddle which has characterized the policy of successive Indian Governments in this area since Independence. In her introduction, Mithu Alur notes that the participants in the seminars from which the book emerged passed a resolution that the education of children with disabilities should be transferred to the Ministry of Human Resource Development (which is responsible for regular education) from the Ministry of Welfare, where it currently resides (Alur 2002a). Though it is not a panacea, I would agree that this seems to be an indispensable first step in overcoming the charitable approach to provision which dominates policy in the country at present, resulting in patchy and inadequate coverage.

It is a pity that there is no concluding chapter. Some attempt to map out priorities for action in response to the many urgent needs identified by contributors, particularly in the first part of the book, would have helped to draw together the disparate threads of argument running through the earlier chapters. Five years elapsed between the seminars which brought the contributors together and the book's publication. In that time, much changed in India in ways which impinge on the prospects for equality of opportunity in its society, not least the resurgence of communalism consequent on the capture of state power by the BJP (Bharatiya Janata Party) in 1998. For this reason, it would have been helpful if a final chapter had been provided which discussed the evolution of social policy in India since 1997. Notwithstanding these reservations, the book is of interest to students and scholars in the fields of comparative education policy and the inclusion of disabled children.

Research and thinking on inclusive education: the state of the field

Summarizing the foregoing section, we can see first of all that work continues to be published which exhibits a large measure of continuity with the major research paradigms which were previously identified. Consequently, it would be incorrect to conclude that these traditions of inquiry had been supplanted. However, in the preceding survey I have updated the map which was drawn in the early 1990s to reveal that a body of work has begun to emerge which adopts a critical perspective towards the inclusion and exclusion of pupils with difficulties in learning in contemporary educational practice, but which eschews the tendencies towards reductionism and determinism which marred earlier work in this field. This work covers an impressive range of substantive foci, including:

- examination of the processes of policy formation at the national and regional level (Booth 1996; Slee 1995);
- deconstruction of the discourses through which identities are constructed (Allan 1996, 1997; Corbett 1996);
- in-depth exploration of the experiences of individual pupils as a stimulus to the investigation of issues of general educational significance (Booth 1996; Hart 1996); and
- excavation of the historical roots of contemporary practice, embracing both the more recent period and the origins of the modern education system (Clark et al. 1997; I. Copeland, 1995, 1996, 1997).

These authors draw on a variety of conceptual frameworks, and it would be a mistake to suggest that there were no differences of outlook between them. Nevertheless, it is possible to identify a number of broad characteristics which are common to this emerging tradition, and which distinguish it from much previous work in the field:

- The research is supported by an evidential base, and analysis proceeds through an engagement with empirical data;
- The analysis draws on critical theory developed in other substantive fields to situate the processes of inclusion and exclusion in a broader social context;
- The authors are apprised of the historically contingent nature of currently dominant forms of practice and patterns of provision, which are not taken as given, but seen as the outcome of a specific process of development;
- The authors do not seek to deny or conceal their own value commitments; specifically, the majority favour a move towards a more inclusive system of educational provision. Though it aims at a rigorous, systematic treatment of the evidence, and acknowledges the need for reflexive self-criticism, this research does not pretend to a spurious impartiality, but acknowledges its own transformative, interventionist intent;
- The narrative constructed through the research is not a linear one (whether of continuous progress or decline), but is alert to the complexity of the flux of historical development, which is always contested, and consequently never entirely predictable, containing many divagations, reversals, and incompletely resolved conflicts.

The research which I have reviewed embodies a struggle to analyse the education of pupils with difficulties in learning as an emergent social practice, which is shaped by the specific historical and cultural conditions in which it takes place, but which cannot be reduced to the mechanical product of forces at work in any other sphere (for example the state of the national economy, or hypostatized traits of the individual psyche), and which single-factor theories are consequently inadequate to account for. As the preceding survey has documented, it has produced a number of substantive additions to the research literature which have advanced thinking in the field.

In Chapters 3 and 4, I present evidence from a study which sought to build on the strengths of this emerging body of work. Like that work, it takes a stance which is both critical and anti-reductionist: critical, in the sense that current educational practices, and the ideologies used to support them, are not taken as given, but seen as the outcome of a specific process of development; and anti-reductionist, in the sense that educational practice as it is manifest in the working life of schools should be seen as a complex and dynamic phenomenon, which cannot be treated as the product of a single determining factor. However, the study also aimed to fill a gap in the literature associated with this outlook, in that the emerging tradition focuses largely on the broad sweep of national policy, or the minutiae of individual interactions and experiences. Whilst accounts based on classroom-level phenomena are not entirely lacking, analyses which focus directly upon the 'meso' level of the institution and offer in-depth, evidence-based accounts of the school development process are as yet less well represented in this body of work.

In the study, I sought to extend the emerging critical, anti-reductionist tradition by directly investigating the processes at work in two English secondary schools where restructuring initiatives were under way, intended to create more inclusive forms of provision. The study used a qualitative, case study approach to gather and interpret evidence on two planes in particular, that is: (i) the organizational structure of provision, especially the provision of support for pupils with difficulties in learning; and (ii) the language used by teachers to discuss pupils with difficulties, and the provision made for them. In both schools, semi-structured interviews were conducted with a cross-section of teaching staff, in which they were asked to describe and comment on the school's provision for special educational needs. Interviews were guided by the following schedule of questions:

1. What do you understand by the terms 'special educational needs', 'pupils with special needs'?
2. How do you aim to meet pupils' special educational needs?
3. Describe how provision for special educational needs is organized in (i) the school; (ii) your department.
4. How effective do you think the school's provision for special educational needs is?
5. How would you like to see the school's provision for special educational needs developed?

The sample was designed to encompass a range of perspectives among the staff, including the coordinators of learning support provision, teachers directly involved in the delivery of learning support, members of the senior management team with salient responsibilities, and a cross-section of teachers from a variety of subject disciplines and with varying levels of experience and seniority. Extracts for analysis were identified in each interview according to their pertinence to the concerns of the study; the data thus obtained was analysed for thematic content using the method of iterative inductive coding, as described in texts on naturalistic methods in social research (Glaser and Strauss 1967; Miles & Huberman 1984; Strauss 1987; Strauss & Corbin 1990). A purpose-built qualitative data analysis software program (QSR NUD•IST) was used to conduct the analysis (see Weitzman and Miles 1995 for a review of this package); the powerful searching facilities provided by this software enabled a fuller, more systematic treatment of the data to be carried out than is typically possible by manual methods. (Further details of the methodology of the study can be found in Skidmore 1998.)

In brief, the study produced evidence of the use by teachers in the same school of different discourses of teaching and learning, which diverged systematically from one another along a number of dimensions. These discourses were articulated by different constituencies of staff, and embodied different visions of the school's past, present and projected future. I also analyse the nature of the relationships between these discourse constituencies, and show that, where divergent discourses co-exist within the same institution, different kinds of relationship may subsist between them.

I believe that the resulting analysis provides a more nuanced theoretical account of the structure of teachers' discourse, on the one hand, and the dynamics of the school development process, on the other, than has hitherto been common in the research literature in this field. Adopting a critical, emergent perspective enables an analysis to be constructed which does full justice to the specificity of the developments under way at each site, whilst at the same time identifying those aspects which are capable of generalization. The major outcomes of the study are twofold:

(i)   a clearer insight into the nature of school development which aims at making provision more inclusive, which can inform the planning and execution of comparable restructuring initiatives in the future; and
(ii) a model of the professional discourse used by teachers in discussing provision for pupils with difficulties in learning, which provides the basis for creating resources to stimulate teachers' continuing professional development, by encouraging them to make their own thinking on these issues explicit, as an aid to critical reflection.

CHAPTER THREE

Downland School: learning difficulties or learning potential?

Downland School, a 13–18 comprehensive of 1300 pupils, is the only second-ary school in a prosperous market town in south-west England. It was formed from the merger of separate girls' and boys' schools in 1992. The headteacher of the new school was formerly the head of the boys' school. He had arrived there in 1988, and the school had seen major changes in staffing, policy and organizational culture since then, which will be described further below. At the time of the study, the school was pursuing a 'total support' model of provision for special educational needs, that is a uniform policy of in-class support with no withdrawal from the mainstream classroom. There were 24 students with statements of special educational needs at the school, all with statements of specific learning difficulties. In the school year in which case study visits took place (1992–93), 50 per cent of pupils aged 15 attained 5 or more GCSE grades A*–C; 95 per cent attained 5 or more GCSE grades A*–G. This placed Downland in the top half of schools in its local authority on this indicator of educational attainment. Because of the demographics of its location, it was subject to little or no effective pressure of competition for pupils with other schools.

As mentioned above, Downland School had been formed from the merger of two previously separate schools, one a boys' school and the other a girls' school. Many of the staff interviewed (from both previous schools) testified that the ethos of the previous schools had been very different prior to the merger, and in particular that they had pursued contrasting policies and practice with respect to special needs provision. Further evidence of this will be presented in the course of the analysis below, but it is pertinent to note at this point that:

- there was a widespread perception among staff from both previous schools that the merger had in fact amounted to a takeover by the boys' school;

- the senior management team of the new school comprised the headteacher and two deputies of the former boys' school, and one deputy from the former girls' school;
- the former boys' school had pursued a policy of total in-class support and no withdrawal for students with difficulties, and students had predominantly been grouped in mixed ability classes;
- the former girls' school had used a mixture of in-class support and withdrawal for one-to-one or small group teaching for students with special needs;
- the head of the team of staff providing learning support in the new school (the teaching and learning coordinator) was a member of the former boys' school staff.

Evidence from a range of staff indicated that the merger had been a difficult experience for many. Staff from both previous schools had had to reapply for their jobs, and a number had been made redundant at the time of merger. A number of interviewees indicated that several staff from the former girls' school had suffered from stress-related illnesses in the period immediately preceding and following the merger.

My analysis will suggest that two discourses could be identified at work in Downland School, which I call the discourse of inclusion and the discourse of deviance (see Chapter 5 for further discussion of these terms). The discourse of inclusion was dominant in the school at the time of the study, in the sense that it was voiced by a number of influential staff (including the headteacher), permeated official school documentation and found support among a significant number of teaching staff, including leaders of curriculum areas. The discourse of deviance was subordinate in the school in the sense that the members of staff most prominent in articulating it were seen by themselves and others as marginalized, and as having little influence over the development of school policy or provision. The fact that these divergent discourses co-existed within the school was acknowledged by many interviewees and, as might be expected from the above account of the origins of Downland, was often linked by them with the merger of the two previous schools with their very different cultures. Research into school development suggests that amalgamation marks a major upheaval in the institutional life of a school (Ball 1987), and there can be little doubt that the merger was indeed an important factor in producing the differences of outlook which were in evidence. However, evidence will also be presented to suggest that, whilst the composition of the constituencies which made use of the divergent discourses overlapped substantially with a division between former boys' and former girls' school staff, it did not wholly correspond with this split, suggesting that the merger cannot be used as a complete and self-sufficient explanation of the observed divergence. Rather, it will be suggested that the merger should be seen as an important factor which contributed to the exacerbation of conflicts and differences of outlook whose roots lie in deeper-seated traditions of beliefs about pedagogy which are held by teachers, and which might be expected to be present in many schools, with or without a history of merger. Although there have been changes in education policy since the fieldwork in Downland School was carried out, the issues raised are of persistent educational import and continue to be relevant to efforts to develop inclusive forms of provision today. They parallel the findings of research concerning the dilemma between equity and effectiveness produced by similar school development initiatives (Avramidis et al. 2002). Further discussion of the general significance of the discourses of inclusion and deviance can be found in Chapter 5.

The discourse of inclusion in Downland: learning potential

In this section, I will describe and illustrate the main features of discourse of inclusion as it was articulated by a range of staff in Downland. It was sponsored by the headteacher and a deputy head, and a major part in its promulgation was taken by the teaching and learning coordinator, whose role will be described in greater detail below. Because of its connection with influential members of staff, it is described as the dominant discourse in the school.

> Where students experience difficulties in learning, it will be necessary to interrogate the curriculum.

This statement, taken from the Teaching and Learning Policy document (originally drawn up in the former boys' school), can be seen as a definitive formulation which encapsulates the discourse of inclusion as it was articulated in Downland. It performs the function of diagnosis or attribution of cause for a phenomenon seen as problematic. In so doing, it simultaneously indicates an orientation towards a mode of intervention or response to this problem, which endorses some kinds of response and tends to rule out others.

A noteworthy feature of the dominant approach to learning support provision in Downland School was the distinctive language in which it was described. There was a conscious use of neologism by several influential figures. The headteacher was quite explicit in this regard:

> What we had to do was *change the vocabulary* in school. It's now become a cliché, of course, . . . So you hear words like 'He's not a problem, he's an opportunity', 'This youngster has a particular facet of his personality that we need to understand', you know, all that kind of stuff.

This account was corroborated by a deputy head from the former boys' school:

> When we talked at any meeting, it was reinforced. In the documentation, . . . It became the *working language*. In a way, there is a lot of humour with it. It was used so often, like *buzzwords*, it became, in a way, a joke but that was good, it was a positive thing not a negative one. Particularly the word 'opportunity' was a real buzzword and it was fun. The fact that it was a joke, it's funny how that humour is quite the thing.

The same interviewee also adverted to the written information ('briefs') supplied to subject teachers about individual students as a second route through which the new discourse was given currency:

> *The language* is in those briefs. Staff found that really useful, some of them particularly found them positively helpful. You know, try this with the student because it has been known to work or let this student work with X student and you will find her much better. It's little practical tips like that. Staff who are hard pressed find that sort of information useful. For some kids, it's very detailed and precise. [The teaching and learning coordinator] would go in and help staff and say try this or that. Support teachers would as well. *The language* was there in that.

According to this interviewee, an important role in promoting the use of the new discourse was also played by members of staff with pastoral responsibilities, particularly the head of year 9 (that is responsible for the new entry year):

> [The head of y9] with her role is very powerful, inducting new students into the school, she uses *that language* about the new students to the staff. They communicated weekly and *that is how she talked* about the students.

We see here the beginnings of the institutionalization of a new way of thinking and talking about the problem of students who, for one reason or another, fail to make the educational progress which might be expected of them, or who underperform in relation to their peers. There is a deliberate rejection of pupil-deficit accounts of learning failure, and a concomitant shift of focus to the curriculum and its adaptation. As the headteacher recalled (describing the change of ethos or culture in the boys' school which he sought to bring about):

> . . . the whole thing about *youngsters who challenge the curriculum* and the monthly staff meetings of an hour and a half were absolutely central in *changing the culture*. So that within a year, staff were beginning to not see the issue as being one of the children being the problem, but them being the problem and how they looked at what they were doing, and beginning to see that you could *approach the problem from a different angle* . . .

For the headteacher, this attempt to shift the ethos was also reflected in a major structural or organizational aspect of provision, namely the organization of a very broad common curriculum for all pupils.

> The other thing we did, particularly for the youngsters who had difficulty with the curriculum as it was structured, we gave them the same curriculum as everybody else. We have an enormous *core curriculum*. We only have one choice really. They all do that. They all do 6 GCSEs. They all are expected to be involved in all activities. We have a jamboree on achievement . . . We have a very clear idea in the school that *you are valued for what you achieve* rather than overall ability.

As can be seen from this account, there is an inextricable connection within the discourse between the stress on the curriculum as the source of difficulties in learning (and, concomitantly, the need to adapt the curriculum in order to preclude such difficulties), and a stress on the educability or positive learning potential of all students. According to this perspective, all students are equally entitled to participate in a common core curriculum, and to be valued for their effort, and for their achievement in the sense of the positive progress that they make, and the skills which they acquire and in which they demonstrate themselves to be competent. This outlook is defined by an explicit contrast drawn with a perspective which is said to value students for their level of innate ability. The stress on the need to reinforce students' self-esteem is equally apparent: that is that all students should be valued by teachers for what they can do and for their progress in learning. Behind this lies the notion that it is mistaken to gauge students according to normative criteria (that is by comparing their level of achievement with those of their peers); rather the aspect of their performance in school which is held out as praiseworthy is their positive accomplishments and how far they have come individually (in comparison with their starting point, rather than with a notional norm of expectation).

Evidence that this discourse was shared by a wider constituency of staff was found, for instance, in the comment of a teacher whose timetable was divided between technology and support:

> What this school offers is a broad, balanced education to all which they seek to extend as far as possible to all students including *atypical students*.

This phrase ('atypical students') provides another example of the 'buzzwords' or neologisms introduced by the teaching and learning coordinator and other proponents of the discourse of inclusion. The phrase would seem to carry the implication that it is the teacher's responsibility to respond to and seek to accommodate the reality of student diversity in their pedagogy (in other words, to find ways of adapting the presentation of the curriculum which facilitate the learning of all students); as opposed, for example, to the notion of 'remediating' the weaknesses of individual students with difficulties.

The embedding of this discourse within the totality of the school's provision was reinforced by the gloss put by the teaching and learning coordinator upon two planned developments of provision, namely: the extension of provision for able students; and plans to monitor and document more precisely the provision experienced by a selection of individual students. On the face of it, it might seem that these two plans for the development of provision stood in contradiction with the emphasis within the discourse on the curriculum as the source of difficulties in learning (as opposed to the individual pupil), and on the equal valuation of all students, regardless of their level of 'ability'. On the contrary, however, the teaching and learning coordinator interpreted the development of provision for more able students as an opportunity to promote the vision of teaching and learning which he promulgated:

> We are extending the able students' project ... This will mean encouraging the staff to use methods appropriate to able students and to use *high order cognition tasks with all students*. This is encouraging because the issue with able students is not generally seen as a problem for

the students, but as *a problem for the curriculum*. More people then, see able students as *a challenge to the curriculum* and are prepared to learn from them and from what they (the teacher) do for them (the students).

He hoped that the able students' project would become a vehicle for encouraging more teachers to adopt the way of thinking about learning which he supported (and its implications for practice), and of extending the scope of this approach to a wider range of students. In this way, it could act as a kind of 'Trojan horse' to get the ideas introduced and acted upon in one area of practice, so that from this established base, their application could be extended to other areas.

A proposed development in the way in which support teachers might operate in the classroom was given a similar interpretation by the teaching and learning coordinator. Although this innovation had not yet been introduced in the school at the time of my visits, it was in fact a development of a method of working which the teaching and learning coordinator himself had previously employed, which was to be extended to incorporate the work of other support staff too. He described the planned addition to the complement of the role of the support teacher as follows:

> Support teachers in each class would identify three students; an able student, an unable student, an odd student. [We] would observe them closely and make close notes on them in terms of two, three or four 'learning competencies' (confidence, motivation, ability to write, to read, to work in a group, to solve problems, to concentrate, to articulate, creativity), then share those notes with the teacher. Then work with the teacher and the students aiming both to observe those competencies in the students and over the next ten weeks to improve them. This means improving the student's work and using them as examples through which *the curriculum and its delivery can be improved*.

As can be deduced from the last comment, the teaching and learning coordinator saw this focus on individual students not as an end in itself, but as a means to the greater end of improving the curriculum. This interpretation becomes more apparent in his account of the planned follow-up to such observations:

> After 10 or 12 weeks, [we would] make further observations to show what the effect has been. These will act as evaluations of process as well as helping the teachers to see when they are doing things well. The effect of this will be, I hope, to *move the emphasis from the student to the curriculum* and will suggest that, though some students are more extreme in their challenges, *the curriculum can adapt and change* so that all students can move forward. It will, I hope, make more of a move towards *treating all students as if they were worthwhile*, and paying attention to all their needs.

At the end of this account, the teaching and learning coordinator again adverts to a principal tenet of the value system to which the discourse appeals for justification: the belief in the positive value and potential of all students.

We may infer that a contrast is drawn with some other philosophies of teaching which (by implication) do not treat all students as if they were worthwhile, and which do not pay attention to the needs of all students. In particular, this position would seem inimical to categorical modes of thinking about students, for example the practice of identifying a certain number of students as having needs that are 'special', set apart from those of the majority.

This last point connects with a second, complementary emphasis of the dominant discourse, whereby all students are viewed as possessed of positive learning potential. To illustrate, in summarizing the philosophy behind the work of the Teaching and Learning Team, the coordinator identified first of all:

> concern that the education of all becomes better; *positive belief in all students*, all teachers; . . .

This echoes the principle repeatedly stressed by the headteacher in interview as central to the 'teaching and learning ethos' of Downland:

> we established a very clear perception of our . . . statements: (1) that *everyone was equal*,

and later:

> The teaching and learning ethos which we have in terms of *equality of opportunity* has been reflected in the pastoral system.

A partially independent corroboration of the widespread acceptance of this outlook was provided by the Coordinator of the Technical and Vocational Education Initiative (TVEI) group in which Downland participated:

> The teaching and learning styles stem from a clear notion of ethos, *parity of esteem* . . . Their concept of special needs will stem from there – it's about each individual student's self-esteem . . . What it's trying to say, . . . fundamentally here is the student at the centre, here are the qualities we're trying to develop, and these are possible ways of getting the student to do that, to become an *autonomous individual with self-esteem*.

Central to this account is the concept of the self-esteem of the learner. In addition to an appeal to abstract notions of rights, the commitment to parity of esteem is justified with reference to an implicit educational rationale: fostering each student's self-image as a successful learner is not only morally proper, it pays dividends in improved learning outcomes. Accounts offered by a number of subject teachers support the inference that this belief in the positive learning potential of all students was accepted by a wide constituency of staff in various curricular disciplines. For example, describing the approach to learning which he sought to encourage among members of his own department, the head of technology commented:

> . . . [I]n general terms *the students are masters of their own destiny*. If they gain trust, they can be left to get on and push forward their own work. I find the kids feed off each other.

In articulating her own pedagogic philosophy, a member of the modern foreign languages department voiced a broad, humanistic definition of education compatible with the idea of enhancing the student's self-esteem as part of educating the whole person:

> You're always telling the individual how well they've done, what they've achieved – I find that almost as important as the information I've tried to pass on to them. *Part of learning is not only learning the subject [but also] that human beings are human.*

A member of the English department began by offering her understanding of the philosophy behind the school's learning support provision:

> Ideally, it doesn't hive off the very able students, it doesn't hive off the . . . the not very clever ones, it *values students individually* – somewhere there is *something they do very well* you have to find, and it might not be very academic,

before going on to describe her own experience as an English teacher, evidence of the value of putting this approach into practice in the classroom:

> I've seen students who . . . do some brilliant stuff, have a really good time, and *be appreciated for things they can do*, and go away feeling that's all right, that they're actually OK as people – not that they're not OK as people because they can't read and write very well.

It is not suggested that the view of all students as possessed of positive learning potential, endorsed within the dominant discourse, was uniformly accepted by all staff; however, these illustrative quotations demonstrate that it existed as more than the rhetoric of members of the senior management team (for instance), since it can be seen to permeate the thinking of teachers from a variety of disciplinary backgrounds, and the language they used when describing and accounting for their experience in the school, and articulating the principles which they sought to realize in their own professional practice.

Another emphasis which was characteristic of the dominant discourse was upon the centrality of staff development in developing a shared school ethos and improving teachers' morale and professional expertise. Describing how he set about reforming the former boys' school on his arrival, the headteacher, for example, said:

> We put an awful lot of money into *staff development*. We put an awful lot of money and time and philosophy into the idea that teaching and learning is central to the school.

This stress on the central importance of staff development in school improvement continued, for him, into the present day:

> If there was something I would want to reflect on that has been going very well, it would be *staff development*. The way we've gone down the road with development plans, sticking to them, being able to enhance people's work through that development has been absolutely central.

A deputy head referred to the fact that all members of the senior management team shared responsibility for staff development as evidence of the central importance allocated to this within the school:

> One of the things we put down on *areas of responsibility* is that all four of us had staff development and that we needed to be aware and have some responsibility for that.

The TVEI coordinator associated with the school provided a quasi-independent confirmation of this perception, paying tribute to the school's continuing investment in staff development, explaining that the school had displayed:

> . . . a great willingness to invest in terms of resources – quite [a] substantial *investment in teaching and learning.*

Another member of the senior management team also stressed that the school was keen to respond positively to requests from staff for support in their professional development where possible. She connected this policy with an ethos of 'openness' in the school:

> We have a very *positive approach to staff development* and staff in the school, if they have a certain request, they usually find they get a positive response about it if it meets the needs of the school and the needs of their career. Again, I think, we go back to this point of being such an *open school* that if somebody does have an area where they feel they are not being developed, I would hope, that they feel they have a chance to say that to any one of us in the senior team. That would be listened to and taken on board.

Further confirmation of this account of the school's support for staff's professional development came from the special educational needs coordinator of the former girls' school. It will be shown below that she was in many ways out of sympathy with the dominant discourse in the school, and felt herself undervalued and marginalized in the development of the school's approach to learning support. Precisely for these reasons, her account of the school's support for her attendance at an external course about dyslexia provides strong confirmation of the claims made by staff who embodied the dominant discourse that the school attached real importance to staff development, which was matched by a willingness to resource individual and collective development activities. Her account also demonstrates that the school provided an opportunity for staff supported in this way to make a contribution to internal staff development, thereby ensuring that skills acquired by staff in external courses were disseminated more widely across the school as a whole:

Interviewer: Is the school supporting you?

Interviewee: They are. I was quite surprised. . . . I went to the head and said could I go and he said it was a good idea. I asked if they would pay and he said OK – it was very cheap.

Interviewer: Are other staff supported in that way at all?

Interviewee: Yes. There is another member of staff who is actually part-time, she is doing the MEd, so we support each other, and yes, I think there are other people. . . . They have asked me to provide some input for a staff day about dyslexia, and that will be interesting to do.

A structural indicator of the importance attached to staff development was the fact that staff meetings in the school were wholly given over to staff development issues and activities. As the headteacher explained:

We had a clear perception of what was expected from staff days – and staff meetings that were *based completely around staff development* so we don't have discussions about little Johnny or anything like that. That isn't on the agenda.

Staff meetings were planned and organized by the Staff Development Group, which was officially coordinated by a deputy head, and chaired by the teaching and learning coordinator. (Further details about the role of the teaching and learning coordinator with regard to staff development will be given below.) The Staff Development Group was also the forum wherein whole school training days were organized. The deputy head gave the following account of its composition and functioning:

Initially, it was any volunteers, anybody who was interested. Then we formalized in that we insisted there had to be a representative of each interest area in the school who acted as a *channel of communication*. In the new [that is merged] school we extended it to include all staff; we had representatives from the support staff, a member of the technician staff and the office staff as well. They are *open meetings*, anybody can come to those meetings. At times it has been a very *powerful group*. It has an agenda and a plan, obviously with the training days, we have these – usually the same – ten staff, meeting [on] training evenings which is a regular pattern of keeping things moving and going and raising issues.

The weight attached to staff development activities in the life of the school was substantially corroborated by a second deputy, whose comments also confirm the consultative mode of operation of the Staff Development Group:

Certainly, I've never been in a school where the staff meetings have been so much *geared towards staff development* and that can only be positive that staff feel that they are getting something out of staff days rather than just purely admin type ones. That takes on board quite a lot of the staff development issues that are coming from the staff themselves, or that the senior people think need to be addressed. I've not worked in a school where there is a staff development group that consists of people from all aspects of the school and *the ideas come from them* rather than just [the teaching and learning coordinator] or [the headteacher] saying we need to do something about an issue. In a way, quite a lot of the needs are met, superficially, by these meetings but then people can take that on further if they feel they want more.

The central significance accorded to staff development was epitomized in a comment made by the deputy head who coordinated the Group's work:

> ... the teaching and learning has become synonymous for us with staff development and planning staff development ...

Within the discourse of inclusion, an organic connection is made between pedagogy, curriculum and staff development; the professional development of teachers, to enhance their ability to vary the presentation of the curriculum by extending the repertoire of methods at their disposal, is seen as occupying a critical place in the task of school improvement (or, in fact, as being equivalent to it). This represents a distinctive interpretation of the nature and purpose of the provision of support for learning, which stands in marked contrast with historically common conceptualizations in which the roots of learning failure are located in the deficits of the individual pupil, and 'support' is defined in terms of remediating the student's weaknesses or difficulties in order to allow them access to a curriculum which does not itself stand in need of any fundamental reconstruction.

A prominent role in promoting the dominant discourse, and the approach to practice endorsed by it, was played by the teaching and learning coordinator. In what follows, I will describe the nature of that role, and the personal style of its incumbent. The post of teaching and learning coordinator had been created during the process of staff restructuring and reorganization which had taken place in the previous five years at the former boys' school. The deputy head with whom the coordinator worked most closely explained how the new post had been tailored to match the strengths of its incumbent, whose potential, in his view, had not hitherto been realized:

> I talked to [the teaching and learning coordinator] with the inspector of the school when I came, who is now in charge of the inspectorate. We said this is a real opportunity here, certainly he was known as a very good class teacher, someone who motivated kids in the classroom.

This account was corroborated by the headteacher, who saw in the coordinator someone capable of acting as an agent of institutional change:

> The key thing for the *change agents*, and the key thing for with [the teaching and learning coordinator] as well was that he suddenly found something to do he could do well, and the second thing was he was encouraged to go out and get on with it. He was given status, not so much financially – a scale, when I came he was on an MPG, he's on a 'C' now ...

The disciplinary background of the teaching and learning coordinator departed from the background of 'specialist' experience in support teaching and special needs work which is typical of many school special educational needs (SEN) coordinators. The coordinator described his own career development as follows:

I came to the job in an odd way. I'm *really a drama teacher*, though, of course, I also teach English. In fact, I've always taught more English. One day (actually several days) I *refused* to let any of my students be taken out to 'special help'. I also *refused* to fill in forms or have support teachers to my lessons unless they helped everyone. I made a fuss and a noise. Anyway, not long after the head of SEN resigned and I was first in line for his job (three or four years ago). Then I did a CAPs [Certificate of Advanced Professional Studies] course and read a lot of books, and so on about SEN. Because *my knowledge comes from books*, because I don't go to local meetings of SEN teachers, and because I get lots of support for the way I do things, *I haven't been socialized yet*.

The coordinator here portrays himself as an outsider to the dominant sub-culture of special needs teaching as it is generally practised. He offers an account of the origins of his distinctive philosophy of how pupils' learning should be supported which presents his views as oppositional from the very outset, defined by resistance to previously prevalent forms of practice (such as withdrawing individual pupils for remedial tuition, and the use of in-class support teaching with identified pupils only). This autobiographical fragment functions, in part, to conjure up a vision of the speaker as a crusader, battling against a widely-accepted tradition of practice which is implicitly seen as unjust or misguided. The coordinator also suggests that his knowledge and thinking about support work have developed in a largely auto-didactic way. During fieldwork visits to the school, he pointed to recent work on 'effective schools for all' (Ainscow 1991c) as being particularly influential in shaping his outlook on provision for special needs (he kept a copy of this book in his office, and referred to it as a source of inspiration). He further defined his own outlook by drawing a contrast with another way of thinking about special needs centred on the notion of students' weaknesses in basic skills which, in his view, was still held by many staff:

The other point of view is that we help students who need help, who can't access the real curriculum because *they don't have the basic skills*. This is a view held by [the former special educational needs coordinator of the girls' school] and lots of people from the old [girls' school] (not just them). It *harks back*, in my view, to remedial teaching, to small groups doing spelling practice in cupboards, and to the idea that some students ('these kids') only and always have special needs which only some special teachers can deal with. It *disempowers* students and teachers. It is always (in my view) patronizing and disabling. It *teaches students to fail* and then tells the students 'I can help you, you need me'!

The strong language used in this description reinforces the interpretation that the coordinator saw himself as involved in a struggle between two irreconcilable points of view, in which he was passionately committed to the victory of his side. An alternative point of view is attributed to other members of staff, in which special needs is conceptualized in terms of deficits internal to the student, which demand specialist expertise on the part of the teacher. This point of view is associated with a past legacy of unsatisfactory provision, in which a narrow, alternative, lower-status curriculum was offered to a minority of pupils, often by withdrawing them for teaching in inferior accommodation. The perspective is portrayed as outdated and oppressive, creating an attitude of dependency in the student, and is ultimately found guilty of causing learning failure. It may be inferred that the coordinator favours a view in which the cause of difficulties in learning is not located within the weaknesses of the individual student; in which responding to the diversity of students' needs is seen as the responsibility of all teachers, and provision for special needs is not the preserve of specialist teachers; and in which all students receive access to a broad curriculum in the mainstream classroom alongside their peers.

A major area of responsibility specifically identified in the teaching and learning coordinator's brief was staff development. This responsibility was exercised through a number of formal and semi-formal aspects of his activity. First, as noted above, he chaired the school's staff development group. In organizing the work of this group, he collaborated particularly closely with the deputy head with senior responsibility for staff development in the school, who described the central role played by the teaching and learning coordinator in the following terms:

> I was the coordinator [of the Staff Development Group] and because of the reasons I talked about, later we asked [the teaching and learning coordinator] to chair the Group. I wasn't going to be seen to front it. [The teaching and learning coordinator] was *managing* the Group because he was destined to do so; he wanted a role. In a way, at the time we gave him his head. He ran the Group, and he still does actually, he helps to *set the agendas*, he works with the Group, *he runs it*. I meet him every Wednesday morning usually to discuss what's happening in school, where we're going and what is there to do. That's what I do now but *he drives it*.

Through chairing the Staff Development Group, the coordinator made a major contribution to the planning and organization of the school's in-service training days. His role was to consult staff about their perceptions of whole school in-service needs before drawing up the agenda for meetings of the Staff Development Group at which the training days were planned. The deputy head with whom he worked most closely described his role as follows:

> [The teaching and learning coordinator] organizes those and *the agenda comes from the staff*. Again, he's very good. What we'd like to do is involve as many staff as possible, it isn't just the group. He asks if anybody would like to help with a certain plan, or he'll know two or three people who have a vested interest and he'll say come and help with this, or to the new staff.

In conjunction with this deputy head, the teaching and learning coordinator also drew up the agenda for weekly staff meetings, which in this school, as was mentioned above, were entirely devoted to staff development activities. The coordinator had also played a 'hands-on' part in leading staff development by making a number of inputs on specific staff development themes at staff meetings and on in-service days. Finally, he was also responsible for consulting with colleagues on an individual basis about their professional development needs, and for negotiating with senior management for school funding to be made available to support teachers who wished to follow external courses of professional development.

The evidence that has been presented supports the inference that the teaching and learning coordinator played a key role in leading professional development within the school. He consulted staff to ascertain their development needs, then, on the basis of this consultation, set the agenda for the staff development group, which in turn organized staff development activities at a whole school level. In this manner, he can be seen as acting as a mediator between the body of the teaching staff and those senior staff charged with formal responsibility for school development matters. This analysis is subject to the qualification that (as mentioned above) meetings of the staff development group were open to all staff for direct participation if they so wished. Nevertheless, it is clear that, as chair of the group, the coordinator exercised a substantial personal influence over the direction of this important aspect of school development. The wry perception offered by a teacher of modern foreign languages, who was in general very supportive of the ethos prevailing in the school, tends to confirm this view:

> It [that is staff development meetings] *seems to have an agenda already . . .* they're run by [the teaching and learning coordinator] and [the deputy head who coordinates the Staff Development Group] and usually [a second deputy head] and a representative of each curriculum area. 'You let them think that they've decided to do it . . .' – I wonder sometimes if our staff development isn't like that!

As was documented above, a high priority was attached to staff development by senior staff in the school, and substantial resources were invested in it, so the coordinator's central role in leading staff development gave him a high profile within the school.

Asked to explain his view of his own role and that of his team of staff (in this school usually called the Teaching and Learning team, rather than the Special Educational Needs department), the teaching and learning coordinator gave a response in which support work and staff development are equated:

> I see the *Special Educational Needs department as a branch of the Staff Development team*. So does the head and [deputy head] who I see as my closest ally. . . . *I think of my job as being Staff Development and Curriculum Development, though I accept that I work through or via those students who most challenge the curriculum.*

The coordinator draws no distinction here between 'special educational needs' work and staff development, defining the two as coterminous. The special educational needs task is reframed in terms of two major areas of whole school development activity (Ainscow 1991c). The formulation is also significant in that it tends to submerge the traditional appeal to individual student characteristics in accounting for difficulties in learning. Where students are referred to, it is through a deliberate neologism ('students who challenge the curriculum') which avoids locating the cause of difficulties within the student and directs attention to the curricular context within which those difficulties manifest themselves. This account also lends support to the view that the discourse of inclusion analysed in the present section was the dominant discourse within the school, in the sense that it was endorsed by powerful figures in the school's staff hierarchy, specifically two key members of the senior management team.

The second major area of responsibility adverted to by the coordinator in the account of his role just cited was curriculum development; this was also a part of the brief given him by senior management. It was formalized in the key part he played in the conduct of departmental reviews (or audits) which were carried out in a rolling programme across the school. His close colleague, the deputy head, explained how the process came about:

> He went into every area and observed them at some length and entered a dialogue with each area. He wrote a paper which then became a sort of *talk of the staff room*. He would report to the management group and we would discuss it with [the teaching and learning coordinator] and the coordinator [of the curriculum area] and that would help them see where they were at and where they might like to go. That was then built into what then became a very formalized development plan for each area.

This description was elaborated by the teaching and learning coordinator, who explained in informal discussion that he was empowered by the senior management team to negotiate access to any area of the curriculum. After reaching agreement with the department in question, he would observe a series of lessons, making notes on semi-structured observation sheets, focusing on the issue of the quality of teaching and learning in the classroom. On the basis of these observations, he would write a short report, highlighting his perceptions of departmental strengths, and areas for development. This report would be used as a basis for discussion at a subsequent meeting between members of the department, members of the senior management team, and the teaching and learning coordinator. The headteacher confirmed the essentials of this account in the following narrative:

> The first area [the teaching and learning coordinator] looked at was science. [He] knows nothing about science and that was his greatest strength. He wrote lots of papers that we used within the area to say 'This is my perception of what is going on in science. You of course may not agree . . .'. He highlighted two areas where we should be concerned, one was science, the other was modern languages.

The deputy head explained how these reviews became formally integrated into the overall enterprise of school development planning, their significance including an impact on resource allocation decisions and target-setting:

> . . . by actually building the work [the teaching and learning coordinator] does with areas into *a plan of development for that area* which becomes quite

precise in terms of what they say they are going to do, in terms of the target and outcomes and the resources we give them, that helps to pin it down as well.

Departments and pastoral teams could also invite the Teaching and Learning team to carry out a review of their work if they felt that they were operating in a reactive, 'crisis management' way:

> When they feel they are *working more as a fire brigade*, they may come to me and we look at the issue with [the teaching and learning coordinator]. 'Why are we acting as a fire brigade in this area, what is going on?' [The teaching and learning coordinator] will go in with his team, observe and start a dialogue in the particular area as to what the issues are and try to tackle it from there. That does have a very powerful thrust.

In reviewing the work of curriculum areas in this way, the teaching and learning coordinator can be seen as acting in the capacity of an internal inspector, or (when invited in by a department) as a consultant. In this role he performs a function of institutional self-evaluation, in which he is concerned directly to examine and appraise a central aspect of the school's activity, the quality of teaching and learning in the classroom, and to offer suggestions for development. A simile used by the headteacher reveals the thinking behind this part of the coordinator's role:

> We used him *a bit like an HMI* and he wrote in the same way, but there was a hidden curriculum in the way he wrote that said to colleagues this isn't going well, that isn't going well and so on.

The overarching aim of the coordinator's role, as identified in his written job description, was to enhance the quality of teaching and learning across the whole school. The foregoing analysis shows that this aim was substantially realized through the leading part he played in two major areas of school development activity, that is staff development and curriculum development, through which he contributed directly to the enhancement of teaching and learning on a school-wide basis. He can be seen to be acting as an evaluator and developer of the processes of teaching and learning within the school.

Another aspect of the role played by the teaching and learning coordinator was his leading part in promoting and making current the discourse of inclusion within the school. Though less formalized than his responsibilities for staff development and curriculum evaluation, this may be judged to be of no less significance in terms of its contribution to engendering a prevalent ethos or culture in the school. Evidence for the significance of his contribution was provided among others by his close collaborator, the deputy head, who attributed the development of the new 'working language' in the school largely to the influence of the teaching and learning coordinator:

> Interviewer: Can I just take you back to the issue of the language that you use in school, where did that come from? How did you evolve the language of 'pupils that challenge the curriculum'?

Interviewee: I must credit [the teaching and learning coordinator] with a lot of it. What we were doing there was when [the teaching and learning coordinator] was describing to us, particularly the work he did around the school in that year he spent going into every class and every area, *the language evolved then.*

The coordinator continued to be seen by many of his colleagues as the leading exponent of the discourse in the newly-merged school, as the following comment by a deputy head (formerly of the girls' school) illustrates:

[The teaching and learning coordinator]'s whole ethos on it is quite refreshing. He *never thinks of 'special needs'*, he says they are *atypical children who challenge the curriculum.*

The headteacher described the functional significance of this aspect of the coordinator's work as follows:

I used to call him the *intellectual conscience of the school.* He'd go in and see something and say 'That's not fair' and then reflect that back to the staff.

Elsewhere he used a related image:

. . . I used [the teaching and learning coordinator] as *a kind of irritant.*

This interpretation was echoed by the deputy head who worked most closely with the coordinator:

[The teaching and learning coordinator] is the *conscience of the school* in a way . . . He carries the message of what the school is about.

In promoting the discourse of inclusion, and the way of thinking about difficulties in learning which it articulates, the coordinator can be seen as a kind of organizational superego, who by his habitual way of looking at things poses a challenge to practices rooted in traditional ideas of special needs education. These accounts also illustrate the contention that the discourse which he helped to create depended for much of its force upon an appeal to essentially ethical positions or matters of value.

The importance of this part of the coordinator's work had been heightened by the recent merger which had brought together two different school cultures. The headteacher saw it as an organizational imperative to ensure that staff from the former girls' school adapted to the new outlook on teaching and learning which had gained currency in the former boys' school, and explained that the coordinator had a 'front line' part to play in this:

The other thing that happened was that [the former girls' school] was still in withdrawal and all that, so that has been the second part of [the teaching and learning coordinator's] role recently, to *bring them into the current way of thinking.* They had to do that. In the beginning some of the [ex-girls' school] staff tried to use methods they'd used before and of course a lot of the kids weren't used to that . . . so they had to adapt.

It will be clear from this analysis that the role adopted by the teaching and learning coordinator represents a considerably broader interpretation of his responsibilities than that associated with the role of the special educational needs coordinator as envisaged in the Code of Practice and related Government guidance (DFE 1994a, 1994b). In particular, the coordinator in Downland was clearly playing a leading part in the process of school development at an institution-wide level; several colleagues saw him as making a significant contribution to the definition and promulgation of the school's culture, through his part in articulating the dominant discourse of inclusion. It is appropriate, therefore, to consider the personal and professional qualities which he brought to bear, and the extent to which his modus operandi was suited to this task of institutional significance.

His colleagues paid tribute to a number of personal and professional qualities which the coordinator brought to the post, and which fitted him to take on an expanded role in the school. Asked to explain why he had elected to cast the coordinator in the role of 'change agent', the headteacher said:

> He's got *an excellent brain*. He's very *up front*. He doesn't mind when people tell him to go away and he'll come back. In a way, he has a very *critical eye for what goes on in the classroom*. He's *non-threatening* to other areas of the curriculum.

A junior colleague from the English department explained how the coordinator was helpful in suggesting alternative approaches in the classroom, or in matters of departmental policy, because of his aptitude for '. . . seeing things from an unusual angle, turning things round.'

Similar attributes of creativity, imagination and vision were ascribed to the coordinator by a deputy head, formerly of the girls' school:

> I think, because [the teaching and learning coordinator] is a *very creative* person, he's *hard to pin down* but also *full of energy* and *great vision* in what he wants to do. He has to be sat down and told that we understand his frustration but if we are going to get anywhere we have to work with the [Learning Support] service.

This description makes it clear that the speaker also sees some potential weaknesses in the coordinator's style, which might be interpreted as the 'flip side' of his personal strengths. An educational psychologist who was employed by the school in a consultative capacity offered further insightful commentary on this issue, that is the interplay between the personal strengths which made the coordinator's approach innovative and original, and certain weaknesses which could spring from these same qualities. A major part of the current focus of her work in the school, she explained, was designed to define more clearly the work of the coordinator and his support team:

> In fact, one of the aspects of what I was here to do when I discussed it with [deputy head] was to help *sharpen up* what [the teaching and learning coordinator's] role actually was. If you are a special needs coordinator and you're fiddling around with individual pupils you know what you're doing, and you're making worksheets and doing programmes, and so on. If you're not doing that, what are you doing? . . . I queried, very early on,

not only what the support teachers were doing but (a) who allocates them in the first place; and (b) who is evaluating or monitoring what they are doing? I'm trying to sharpen up that whole area. [The teaching and learning coordinator] responded by sending them out a letter asking 'What do you think you're doing?' and he's only just got some replies back to act on. I asked if he had termly meetings with them to make sure that something is happening other than dealing with things by throwing a support teacher at them. He is so much on *the principle of people working out what they do for themselves*, which is fine, but I keep telling him that he is there to *enable them* to be able to do that and to *facilitate them* doing that, not just to say 'I don't know, go away and work it out!'. I think that's a thing that should happen more often, the meetings between the support teacher, the class teacher and [the teaching and learning coordinator]. Those triads should happen more often. They hardly happen at all. Some of them are a real mismatch of expectations.

She summed up her concerns about the coordinator's working style as follows:

. . . *he works on the assumption that folks go away and do it.* I keep telling him that they're *waiting for some guidance* on it and support in their doing it – even if it's a termly pat on the back. It's so woolly in some of the instances . . . He so *'overviews'* things that the nitty gritty he assumes everybody is doing.

Related concerns are apparent in the following comments of a member of the senior management team (which at the same time pay tribute to the coordinator's energy and commitment):

[The teaching and learning coordinator] is *not a form filler*, he's someone who just wants someone to come in and help the child, *forget the paperwork*, don't waste time, just do it.

The picture of the coordinator which emerges from these accounts is of someone who has many positive strengths which equip him to make a significant contribution to shaping the direction of the school's development (in conjunction with members of the senior management team who supported his work). The same qualities which fitted him to take on this institutional development role (for example creativity, the ability to take a strategic view, original insight) were associated with characteristics which raised concerns about his formal responsibility for organizing the work of his team of support staff (for example a reluctance to provide explicit guidance, impatience with matters of administration and record-keeping, a possible lack of clarity about the precise extent of his own responsibilities and those of his team).

The foregoing analysis has documented the use in Downland of a discourse of inclusion, which was deployed by a significant constituency of staff across a number of curricular areas, who occupied a range of positions in the school's staffing structure. It has been demonstrated that this discourse was dominant in the school in the following senses: its usage was endorsed by several powerful senior members of staff whose views were instrumental in shaping the school's ethos or culture (for example the headteacher and other members of the senior management team); it informed the official language of school policy, being found in the school's public policy documents; and it coincided with a number of key, distinctive aspects of practice and provision (for example the exclusive use of staff meetings for staff development purposes, or the work carried out by the teaching and learning coordinator in an internal curriculum evaluation role). The structure of the dominant discourse of inclusion in Downland School was articulated along the following dimensions, each of which has been illustrated in the actual utterances of teachers quoted above:

- The source of students' difficulties in learning is to be found in deficiencies in the way in which the curriculum is presented to them (rather than in their innate weaknesses or lack of ability);
- In responding to students' difficulties in learning, the school's teaching staff should seek to improve the presentation of the curriculum by developing their pedagogy (rather than attempting to remediate students' weaknesses in basic skills);
- A positive student identity is constructed which represents all students as possessed of the potential to learn (in contrast to the practice of identifying a discrete sub-group of 'special needs' students, defined in terms of their negative characteristics);
- All students are to be valued equally for their achievements and for the progress which they make in learning (students should not be valued differentially according to their innate levels of ability);
- The use of neologisms (such as 'students who challenge the curriculum') is encouraged in order to foster attitudes which problematize the curriculum rather than the student (conventional ways of speaking which appear to locate the cause of difficulties within the individual student are discouraged, for example phrases such as 'students with special needs');
- The professional development of teaching staff is to be seen as central to the improvement of curriculum and pedagogy throughout the school by enhancing the repertoire of methods at teachers' disposal;
- The organization of the school's provision is to be justified by appeal to the values of equity and justice (rather than by pragmatic, case-by-case decisions about the kind of provision which is judged to be in the interests of the individual student);
- All students are entitled to participate in a broad, common, core curriculum and experience success in that curriculum (rather than the provision of an alternative curriculum for students with special needs with a narrow focus on basic skills);
- As a matter of principle, the location of support teaching should be within the regular classroom (students with difficulties in learning should not be withdrawn to be taught separately from the rest of the class);
- The purpose of 'support' work is to secure improvements in teaching and the presentation of the curriculum (not to remediate the weaknesses of individual students);

- The role of the coordinator of teaching and learning is defined in terms of operating at a whole school level to bring about improvements in curriculum and pedagogy, and in terms of operating at a deep cultural level to engender a new school ethos. (It is not to be equated with the role of the special educational needs coordinator where this is defined in terms of identifying and assessing individual students with special needs, record-keeping and administration, or the direct tuition of individual students with difficulties.);
- All teachers are seen to be responsible for the teaching of all students (there is not a distinct category of students whose education is the province of teachers with specialist expertise in special educational needs); and
- The agenda for joint meetings of teaching staff should focus on whole school staff development issues (not on discussion of the problems of individual students).

The discourse of deviance in Downland: learning difficulties

Not all teachers at Downland School shared the outlook on student learning adumbrated above. Analysis revealed a second, contrasting discourse in use, which articulated a sharply opposed set of views about the nature of students' difficulties in learning and the provision which should be made in response to such difficulties. In this section I will illustrate this perspective, which I call the discourse of deviance (see also Chapter 5). A key property of the discourse of deviance is its affirmation of the centrality of the interests of the student in determining questions of practice or provision. To this extent, it carries echoes of the ideology of 'child-centred' education which became widely influential in British primary practice from the 1960s on. A clear illustration of this component of the discourse was furnished by the comments of a member of the Teaching and Learning team, who had previously been the special educational needs coordinator at the former girls' school. For example, when speaking about her contribution to the extension project for able students, which involved giving up lunchtimes and work after school, she summed up her philosophy as follows:

> I just feel very committed to *those students; that's my focus.*

Elsewhere, she described how she had recently been made responsible for pupils with statements, but had been refused a concomitant increment in salary (or 'responsibility point'), adding however:

> But then I'm that sort of person, I suppose, I accept things and am philosophical about them because I think *it's the kids that matter most.*

The value system to which the discourse makes appeal in justifying the vision of education it embodies (what might be called its underlying axiology) can thus be interpreted as an appeal to the centrality of the interests of the pupil, as these are construed by the teacher.

Closely associated with the notion of the centrality of the student is a construction of the student's identity in terms of the difficulties of which they are possessed. The student is typically defined in terms of those things which they cannot do or which they have problems with (what has been called a 'child-deficit' view of special needs; Ainscow 1991b: 216). The same interviewee, for example, supported her argument for 'case conferences' about individual students as follows:

> In fact, it's something I'm a great believer in, if we get the *students with difficulties* sorted out and develop strategies for them, we can apply those strategies elsewhere,

continuing:

> I think there's a lot that can be applied. I think when you are working *one to one* or with *small groups of students* you become very aware of the sorts of processes that are going on, the *sorts of difficulties that they have* with either understanding work or presenting work or having study skills. . . . You become more aware of the other *students as individuals*, and I think that's vitally important for motivation and stimulation. *They must be regarded as individuals*, and even if you're talking to them as a group, they must feel that you are speaking to them individually.

This account also serves to illustrate another characteristic emphasis of the discourse, viz. the stress it places upon the student *as an individual*. Formally, there might appear to be consensus between the two discourses on this proposition, since I showed above that the discourse of inclusion emphasized the importance of valuing all students equally; however, the implications for practice which are drawn within each discourse stand in marked contrast to one another. On the one hand, the discourse of inclusion goes on to argue the need for teachers to vary their teaching methods in order to build a curriculum suited to the reality of student diversity; whereas the discourse of deviance maintains a focus on the individual student as the source of the problem, and advocates a form of intervention aimed at overcoming the weaknesses which prevent them from participating in a mainstream curriculum which is assumed to remain unreconstructed in its fundamentals. The difference in orientation was reflected in the former special educational needs coordinator's view that withdrawing the student for one-to-one work could be beneficial in some cases (rather than operating a policy of 'total support' with a blanket ban on withdrawal):

> I think . . . it has always been recognized that a *one to one situation is quite effective* although there's been this thrust of working with these children in the classroom. I think that depends; in some situations it works extremely well and you can *support the child* very effectively in the classroom, but sometimes it's an embarrassment for them to have you there. They don't concentrate and so a way of encouraging concentration is to take them away.

Echoes may be detected in these comments of the appeal to 'benevolent

humanitarianism' which Tomlinson identified as the ideology used to legitimate the practice of segregation in special education (Tomlinson 1982). The
former special educational needs coordinator's explanation of a major source
of job satisfaction for her also carries echoes of this humanitarian rationale:

> *I get a lot out of working with them* [that is individual students with difficul-
> ties]; a lot of *positive feedback from them*, positive feedback from the
> teachers who work with them, and we meet and discuss informally. I also
> get positive feedback from their parents when they speak to me on the
> phone or come and see me.

This comment takes us on to a final aspect of the 'individual focus' of the
discourse of deviance, namely the way in which it is characteristically articulated in terms of episodes of interpersonal interaction, rather than through
discursive arguments appealing to abstract ideas or theoretical concepts. It is
common within this discourse for the speaker to narrate an incident or episode
of one-to-one interaction with another teacher or a pupil, drawn from their
professional experience in their working life; this account then serves as an
illustrative example of the importance of the values endorsed by the discourse,
or in other words as a kind of pedagogical parable (Shulman 1986), carrying an
implicit evaluative message which may not be fully spelt out. An example is
found in an anecdote narrated by the former special educational needs
coordinator to illustrate the principle that, in the coordination of support
teaching, the student for whom support is being provided should be explicitly
identified, and an opportunity should be made for teachers who work with the
student to discuss support strategies appropriate for that individual (both of
these suggestions were counter to prevailing practice in the school):

> I had *a talk* with [a member of the school's learning support team] this
> morning *about a student* that he works with some time in the week and I
> work with. He has had a new statement through and so we made time this
> morning to talk about him and to talk about the way that he was support-
> ing him and the way I was supporting him. It's like a *mini case conference*
> but it would have been nice to have more staff there to listen and hear
> their input.

It can be seen that this mode of reasoning articulates a discursive world popu-
lated by concrete examples of 'good practice', that is first-hand accounts of
interactions narrated by the speaker which demonstrate or exemplify the
pedagogical values endorsed within the discourse of deviance, thereby negat-
ing the appeal to abstract principles which characterizes the discourse of
inclusion.

Another important distinguishing characteristic of the discourse of deviance, related to its articulation through pedagogical parables, is its axiological
appeal to pragmatism, that is the ultimate value system to which reference is
made in advocating or criticizing a specific form of practice or provision is the
notion of 'what works'; this is the litmus test which is applied within the
discourse in evaluating the current organization of provision in the school,
and in justifying proposals for changes in practice. This underlying axiology

stands in marked contrast to the strong emphasis placed in the discourse of inclusion upon affirmations of principle or notions of students' rights as the point of reference in forming evaluative judgements about current provision or changes in practice that are needed (for example value positions such as equality of opportunity, or the need to value all students equally).

This difference was perhaps most forcibly expressed in comments made by the former special educational needs coordinator from the girls' school, in contrasting her own approach with that of the teaching and learning coordinator:

> I think, sometimes, [the teaching and learning coordinator]'s dynamism is regarded as a bit 'over the top'. I mean *there is a lot of theorizing but it's the practicalities that people want to get down to*. I know – I talk to a lot of staff, not necessarily about [the teaching and learning coordinator], but they want to know *what they can do to help*.

Elsewhere she described how:

> There's this sort of disparity, I think, between *looking at a pupil's difficulties* and trying to help them *work round it* and *come to terms* or find a *strategy for coping*, and this idealism, which I think [the teaching and learning coordinator] has, of the ideal situation.

The poles of this 'disparity' draw a clear contrast between an approach which is seen as idealistic but impractical, predicated on abstract principles, and the speaker's own approach where the basic ontological reality is the difficulties of which the student is possessed, and the goal of intervention is to help the student find a means of circumventing or accommodating to these recalcitrant features of their identity.

An English teacher who was formerly a member of the girls' school echoed this point of view. She explained how, in the former girls' school, pupils with special needs were sometimes withdrawn from lessons. Since the merger of the two schools, this practice had been discontinued; commenting on this (the policy of 'total support') she explained that she was not opposed to the use of in-class support teaching, but felt that the targeting of in-class support, and the use made of it, were not working coherently across the school, adding that in her view:

> . . . we need to talk more about devising *systems that will actually work*, rather than everybody doing their own thing.

She also drew a rueful contrast between the dominant ethos of continuously reinforcing pupils' self-esteem, and the pragmatic need of the classroom teacher to use disciplinary sanctions against pupils who failed to submit work which had been set:

> *On the one hand* you've got the head of year telling them they're all wonderful in assembly, *and then* that afternoon you're handing out report slips to kids because they're not handing their homework in, and *it's the balance of those two that sometimes goes a little awry.*

A further example of the appeal to pragmatism in justifying a model of peda-gogical practice was furnished by the former special educational needs coordinator's elaboration of the need for 'flexibility' in the use of the strategies of withdrawal and in-class support; as was indicated above, she firmly believed that both options should be available to the supporting teacher. (Her com-ment also illustrates once again the central importance attached to the interests of the individual pupil within this discourse.):

> It depends on the student and the situation so you have to be flexible enough to be able to take advantage of whatever situation is going on and turn it to the best advantage for that particular student.

Something of the same outlook would also seem to underlie her advocacy of a 'holistic' approach to provision for special needs in general:

> It's no good working on a 'problem' or an idea or a project with just one approach – you've got to have, I think, *a holistic view of what it is you want to achieve*, and then *you've got to try all different sorts of things to get there*. . . . I think the *multi-faceted approach* [is needed], – this idea that it is a con-tinuum that will somehow meet in the middle is just two-dimensional.

Another way of describing this point of view is pluralistic eclecticism: the speaker rejects the idea that there is a single, monistic philosophy which can be used to guide the development of provision, in favour of teachers trying out a multiplicity of different methods in a non-dogmatic way, to find out 'what works' best in practice.

One elision, or significant silence, which may be detected in the discourse of deviance is that speakers often omit to mention or make explicit the cri-teria by which a form of practice or provision can be judged to have 'worked'. By inference from the 'diagnosis' of difficulties in learning arising from weaknesses internal to the individual pupil, we may deduce that the criterion of whether an intervention has worked must be whether the dif-ficulties attributed to the pupil have been overcome or remediated. If an intervention does indeed succeed in lessening the difficulties experienced by an individual student, then it may be possible to extend its application to other cases. The development of provision for students with difficulties in learning, then, is seen essentially not as a systemic, institution-wide task requiring the examination of curriculum and pedagogy across the school, but as the aggregate outcome of a constellation of individual interventions with pupils on a case-by-case basis. As a corollary of this perspective, doubt is cast on the value of 'theoretical' and 'idealistic' ideas about how teaching and learning in general might be improved, which is the ground on which the dominant discourse of inclusion is built. It is as if the two discourses were looking at schooling through opposite ends of the telescope: one which brings into focus questions of the organization and quality of provision across the whole school for all students; and the other which narrows the aperture to focus upon each student with difficulties in learning as an indi-vidual case to be remediated discretely. The two orientations are counter-posed to each other in the contradictory constructions which they make of the nature and causes of difficulties in learning among students, and in the appropriate form of provision which should be made in the school in response to such difficulties.

A particularly clear example of the contrast in orientation between the two discourses is furnished by the difference of opinion over the practice of 'case conferences'. The former special educational needs coordinator of the girl's school explained that she had proposed the idea of holding regular timetabled case conferences between support staff and subject teachers to discuss individual students with whom both sets of staff worked. Initially, senior staff associated with the dominant discourse of curriculum development had poured cold water on this proposal:

> That's why I suggested that we use assembly time for these *case conferences* but the head said that it's not important enough as there are too few students involved.

More recently, however, there had been a shift of position:

> I wanted to set up a morning meeting in a sort of *case conference format about individual students*, and that was squashed, but it has now been supported that we can do that.

Her account of the initial resistance to her idea would seem to be consistent with the headteacher's account (cited earlier) of the exclusive thrust of school staff meetings towards professional development:

> We had . . . staff meetings that were based completely around staff development so *we don't have discussions about little Johnny or anything like that.* That isn't on the agenda.

The rationale advanced by the former special educational needs coordinator to support the need for case conferences is founded upon two key principles: the need for a 'consistent' or 'coherent' approach (among various teachers involved in supporting individual students with difficulties); and the value of 'pooling' or 'sharing' information and ideas. These points of reference can be seen in the following account which she offered of a meeting which she had just held with a subject teacher to discuss a particular pupil with whom they both worked:

> It's so important to have some sort of *consistency* and, while it doesn't impede you using something which might be an innovation or revelation by knowing that you've got the facility to *group people together to talk about that particular student*, you could *pool* those resources and *share those ideas*; you could be more effective in fact. We both found that very valuable. It's not that we are doing different things, we are doing very much the same things, but knowing that gives us more confidence to carry on with what we are doing.

Similar points of emphasis can be found in her response when asked to describe how she would like to see the school's provision for students with learning difficulties develop. The desideratum which she identified was the need to hold regular meetings of all support teaching staff in order to promote greater 'coherence':

I think I'd like more *coherence*. I'd like – yes, we have a meeting every half-term for the support staff, but because a lot of them are part-time they quite often don't all come because they're not in on the particular day we have the meeting. I think it's really important to have that *coherence* with the group so that we have some sort of input – some sort of INSET – on whatever to keep up to date with various methods of support; time to *pool our ideas*, time to have *case conferences* so that if two or three of us are working with *a particular child* because of timetable constraints, that we actually *pool the information*.

Evidence that the former special educational needs coordinator's practice conformed to this modus operandi, insofar as she was able to implement it, was provided by a non-teaching assistant whose main responsibility was to support identified individual students with a statutory statement of special educational needs, who described how she wrote lesson reports on individual students for her:

Every lesson I have to write a small report which goes to [the former special educational needs coordinator] of the school, and she coordinates that – basically what the lesson was like, what was he asked to do, how did he respond – there is a list. I will ask questions [on the lesson report] – I had this problem, what do you think I should have done with it? . . . Then as I see her in the school, she'll say, 'About this problem, I think this is the best way'.

It will be apparent that the practice of holding 'case conferences' (and related forms of provision) tends to shift the focus of professional exchanges between teachers and support staff on to the theme of individual students, their difficulties in learning and the strategies used by staff to support them. This stands in contrast to the focus of the dominant discourse of inclusion upon the themes of the curriculum and pedagogy provided for all students throughout the school. Case conferences are consistent with the 'theory of causation' of learning difficulties described above which locates the source of difficulties in the deficits of the individual student. The 'terms of reference' envisaged for them circumscribe the individual student as the cause for concern to be addressed, thereby tending to rule out of consideration the nature and quality of the curriculum which the school presents to all pupils. This is justified by an appeal to the need for a consistency of approach (which, in this context, is used to designate the consistency of the methods used to support the learning of an individual student with difficulties by different staff involved in teaching him or her).

This analysis would seem to raise a significant paradox or contradiction *within* the discourse of deviance. On the one hand, as noted above, the discourse appeals to the notions of 'flexibility' and 'pragmatism', for example in justifying the need for remedial teaching in a withdrawal situation to be available as an option. (By inference, the discourse of inclusion stands accused of inflexibility and idealism in its insistence upon a blanket policy of no withdrawal.) On the other hand, as we have just seen, the discourse of deviance also makes appeal to the need for greater 'consistency' and 'coherence' in justifying the need for case conferences among staff about individual students with difficulties. (By implication, the dominant discourse is guilty of fostering inconsistency and incoherence through its refusal to countenance joint discussion among staff which focuses upon individual students.) In other words, in criticizing the current state of provision and putting forward proposals for alternative forms of practice, the discourse of deviance appeals at one and the same time both to the need for greater *flexibility* and to the need for greater *consistency*; the discourse of inclusion is accused simultaneously of the faults of inflexibility and inconsistency. The difference of emphasis between the two discourses is in any case quite marked at this point. The specific issue of case conferences (about individual pupils) vs. staff meetings based around staff development (where 'little Johnny' is not on the agenda) raises once again in a new guise the broader questions of the nature and causes of students' difficulties in learning, and the form of provision which should be adopted in response to them. In other words, it raises the question of whether the structures and institutionalized practices of the school should be organized primarily to promote the sharing of information about individual students with difficulties, and the strategies used by their teachers; or whether they should be geared primarily towards problematizing and interrogating matters of general pedagogical significance, affecting the quality of teaching and learning for all students throughout the school. On this question, as before, the two discourses face in opposite directions: each takes a different primary concern as its point of departure, which in turn leads to divergent forms of practice being endorsed by each discourse.

A further differentiating characteristic of the discourse of deviance is the emphasis it places upon the importance of teaching students basic skills which are seen as prerequisites to enable them to access the regular curriculum. This point was identified by the teaching and learning coordinator as marking an important distinction between the approach for which he stood, and the views of some other staff:

> The other point of view is that we help students who need help, who *can't access the real curriculum because they don't have the basic skills*. This is a view held by [former special educational needs coordinator at girls' school] and by lots of people from the old [girls' school] (not just them).

Some evidence to support his assessment is found, for example, in the comments of a teacher of modern foreign languages who had been at the boys' school for four years prior to the merger, and was in general supportive of its 'positive' ethos and the stress on students' potential:

> I find that the *'weak'* ones are much better with their listening *skills*. . . . The goodies have got to go through and achieve GCSE and the others have got to at least feel they've achieved something. Usually they divide themselves . . . but not always 'goods' and 'weaks' – there's very often a mixture

... We went purposely for doing everything on a sheet because it is *a weak student who has reading problems* who has battled with the first sheet to find what book they've got to go to – they've given up. With the writing we've always tried to make it so that *a student who has writing problems* can get away with about one word, but then the stronger ones have got the chance to let them flow.

This teacher was committed to the department's policy of flexible learning (realized in part through the development of a large bank of differentiated worksheets), a policy which was consistent with the stress on curriculum differentiation and in-class support associated with the discourse of inclusion. However, the formulations used in this description contain many elements reminiscent of the emphases of the discourse of deviance, including a rough typification of students according to levels of ability ('goods' and 'weaks'), an identification of the student according to the nature of the difficulties of which they are possessed ('a student who has reading/writing problems'), and a reference to basic language skills (listening, reading and writing), weakness in which is seen as a constraint upon the student's effective participation in this area of the curriculum.

An extended account which draws on the notion of basic skills was offered by the former special educational needs coordinator of the girls' school in commenting upon the school's provision for students with specific learning difficulties. (It will be recalled that all the school's students with statements of special educational needs (24) were identified as having specific learning difficulties. The question of how their learning should be supported was therefore of considerable significance for the school's provision for special needs.) A major strategy employed with many of these students, which was demonstrated and explained by the teaching and learning coordinator, consisted in supplying them with 'notepad' computers (small laptop machines) equipped with software designed to assist with writing problems (including a spellchecker). The former special educational needs coordinator questioned the wisdom of relying on this strategy as much as the school did, to the exclusion of practice in more fundamental skills:

> The resourcing thing, yes, it's useful to be able to let students have notepad computers and dictaphones and any other sort of equipment that they want but it has inherent difficulties and problems because those students (a) have to be encouraged to bring them; (b) to use them; and (c) they have to be maintained in good working order to use them efficiently. You have to *instruct them in their use* so, again, it's added input. A lot of them *don't have typing skills* so they don't know how to use them. So there are bonuses and there are negatives. ... I also wonder whether giving some students a notepad computer just because they have dyslexia-type problems is the ideal solution or whether it creates more problems for them in that, I think, that sometimes *practising handwriting fluency* is actually helping them establish a pattern. It's something that is used as an approach, and so you have to juggle those things. You have to make sure that sometimes they have had *writing practice* and they get used to taking

notes, because that again is another *skill* and they should be *practising*. Also *they need the skills* to be able to use the equipment they are given effectively. Again, it's added input and while you are concentrating on *giving them the skills* for those, while it might be more productive in the *long run*, in the *short term* while they are focusing on *acquiring those skills*, there are *other skills that they are not acquiring.*

In this account, an element of current provision is criticized on the grounds of the students' lack of the requisite skills, and the consequent need for teachers to instruct them in this extra set of skills ('added input'). An alternative approach is commended because it enables the students to acquire and practise other, more basic skills (especially writing skills) in which they are deficient, and which are seen both as inherently important, and as necessary prerequisites to allow them to access the mainstream curriculum. A contrast is also drawn between skills in the use of technology, which may be of long-term value, and the practical skills which students urgently need to acquire in order to participate successfully in the mainstream curriculum. This account can also be seen to reinforce the student-deficit model of the origins of learning difficulties, in that students are described in terms of skills which they need to acquire, and which, it is consequently implied, they do not currently possess, or do not possess to the requisite level; it is the students' deficiencies in skill acquisition which create the obstacle to learning which must be overcome (not, for example, deficiencies in the manner in which teachers present the curriculum to them). In contrast to the emphasis placed in the discourse of inclusion upon the positive capability of all students to learn and achieve success in the mainstream curriculum, within the discourse of deviance students are commonly identified in terms of those things which they cannot do, or cannot yet do.

Some evidence was found to permit a final component of the discourse of deviance to be identified. Comments made by some subject teachers which were consistent with the view of difficulties in learning found within this discourse suggest that they were inclined to adopt a different conceptualization of the nature of teachers' pedagogical expertise from that endorsed by the discourse of inclusion. In our analysis of that discourse, we saw the importance attached to the professional development of staff, with a particular emphasis on the extension of the repertoire of methods at their command; an emphasis which carries the implication that teachers' pedagogical expertise resides centrally in their ability to adapt curriculum and pedagogy to suit the diversity of students' learning needs. A rather different notion of the main source of teachers' pedagogical expertise is found in the comments of a science teacher (formerly a member of the staff of the girls' school) in describing her reservations about the idea of providing differentiated work within the classroom:

I think science teachers tend to want to *structure* . . . we have safety considerations other people don't have . . . and that perhaps limits our views of what different approaches we can take . . . In science especially *you've got a subject to deliver, a topic*; therefore you put together *the work that you need to cover*, and assume, or hope, that everybody will get through it to some extent or other, but *you can't really give that much thought to totally different activities for parts of the class.*

This account constructs the notion of a subculture peculiar to science as a subject; science is defined as a subject specialism. This view is justified partly on pragmatic grounds ('safety considerations'), but more fully by articulating a view of the curriculum centred on the teacher's subject-specific content knowledge ('a subject . . . a topic'). It is in their possession of this knowledge that teachers' pedagogical expertise is seen to lie; a source of expertise which is explicitly prioritized above the need to provide differentiated learning activities for the range of students within the class. There is an explicit appeal to the metaphor of teaching as the transmission of content knowledge ('you've got a subject *to deliver*') which is placed in antithesis to the emphasis of the discourse of inclusion on modifying the curriculum and its presentation to suit the range of student needs. Some corroboration of this outlook is found in an account of support teaching in the modern foreign languages department provided by a member of that department who was formerly a member of staff at the boys' school. In contrast to the practice prevailing throughout the rest of the school, all support teaching in this department was provided by other subject specialists (linguists). The teacher stressed the value of this policy, saying:

> At the moment we've got *always linguists* with us on support . . . *Working with other language teachers as support teachers is very good*, because you do pick up other ideas then.

She felt that this benefit would only be likely to arise when working alongside other linguists who shared a common specialist knowledge of their subject. The emphasis in these comments on the central importance of specialist subject knowledge in defining the nature of teachers' pedagogical expertise stands in contrast to the central importance in the discourse of inclusion attached to teachers' ability to differentiate the presentation of the curriculum in defining the nature of their pedagogical expertise.

In this section, I have shown that a second discourse was in use among some teachers in Downland, which encapsulated an outlook upon schooling which departed significantly from that presented within the discourse of inclusion. The most prominent exponent of this discourse of deviance was the former special educational needs coordinator of the girls' school, but (as the analysis has shown) several important components of the discourse were shared by a range of other teaching staff. Whereas the discourse of inclusion was described as dominant in defining the ethos of the school, the discourse of deviance occupied a subordinate position, in the sense that it was predominantly voiced by members of staff who felt themselves to be marginalized within the new, merged school. They were generally in low-status positions in the school's staffing structure, and their views had little impact on shaping institutional policy, or informing official school policy documents. The structure of the subordinate discourse of deviance is summarized below:

- The source of students' difficulties in learning is to be found in weaknesses or problems which are attributes of the student (rather than in the manner in which the curriculum is presented to him/her);

- In responding to students' difficulties in learning, teachers should seek to remediate the student's weaknesses or help the student to circumvent them (as opposed to interrogating the mainstream curriculum);
- All students should be treated as individuals, with the corollary that some may need differential treatment from that provided for the majority through the mainstream curriculum. (The idea that all students are equally capable of learning successfully in the mainstream curriculum is naive or idealistic.);
- Provision for students with special needs should aim to equip them with the basic skills which are prerequisites for successful participation in the mainstream curriculum (in contrast to the provision of a common curriculum which is the same for all students);
- The facility to withdraw students with difficulties for one-to-one or small group tuition should be available as an option. (The policy of exclusive use of in-class support teaching is inflexible.);
- Teachers who provide learning support should be encouraged to hold case conferences about individual students with difficulties and the strategies which can be used to support them (in contrast to the prevailing policy of staff meetings which were wholly devoted to general staff development issues);
- The evaluation of provision for students with special needs should be governed by considerations of pragmatism, 'what works' for individual students (rather than by appeal to abstract values such as equity, 'what is fair');
- The discourse is articulated through the recounting of pedagogical parables which narrate episodes of interpersonal interaction epitomizing examples of 'good practice' (instead of through appeal to universal principles and the coining of neologisms);
- Teachers' pedagogical expertise is seen to reside centrally in their possession of specialist subject knowledge (rather than in their ability to vary the presentation of the curriculum).

Relationships between the discourses

I have already noted that the discourse of inclusion occupied a position of dominance in Downland School, in the sense that it was used by a constituency of staff which included the majority of the senior management team, and other staff influential in implementing aspects of whole school policy (such as the teaching and learning coordinator); it also formed the 'official language' of school policy, found in formal documents such as the Teaching and Learning policy. Correspondingly, the discourse of deviance occupied a subordinate position in the school, in that it was associated with a constituency of staff who felt themselves (and were perceived by others) to be marginalized, exercising little influence on school policy or the development of provision. In the final part of this chapter, I will illustrate and explore the nature of the relationships between the two discourses in greater detail.

Conflict and domination

I think *the schools were very different in terms of ideology*, and there is definitely a *dominating [boys' school] factor*.

[English teacher, former boys' school]

The existence of fundamentally opposed views among staff about teaching and learning was no secret in Downland; indeed, it was openly remarked upon by a number of interviewees with differing perspectives, including the teacher cited above. It will be recalled that Downland School was formed from the recent merger of previously separate girls' and boys' schools; unsurprisingly, many teachers pointed to the history of amalgamation in accounting for differences in philosophy in the new school. For instance, a female deputy head, formerly from the girls' school, commented:

It is interesting coming from another school where there's *a very different culture – totally different.* . . . They were just *standing at opposing points of the world*, basically.

One member of the modern foreign languages department, undertaking initial teacher education through the licensed teacher scheme, was a beginning teacher in the newly-merged school, and may therefore be taken as a relatively impartial witness in that he had not been a member of the staffs of either of the previous separate schools. He had found that:

Teaching methods were different at the two schools, I believe . . . you have very passionate arguments about it.

Studies of school amalgamation show that the process generally creates 'winners' and 'losers' in terms of status, responsibility and influence, which may lead to a pattern of polarization in the aftermath of merger (Ball 1987); Downland was no exception to this rule. One locus of antagonism where the lines of conflict were particularly clearly drawn was the English department. The head of department in the new school was the former head of English in the boys' school; the head of English from the girls' school became second in department following the merger, an effective demotion which he greatly resented. Overlaid on these personal rivalries were deep-seated ideological disagreements about teaching methods and pupil grouping arrangements. A rift had developed between the former boys' school staff, who were strong supporters of mixed ability teaching, and teachers from the girls' school, who were advocates of streaming. An English teacher from the former boys' school explained:

[The head of English], our department leader, is really adamantly mixed ability, and I agree with him entirely . . . we met the [girls' school] staff, and I'm sorry to say, they are for quite rigid streaming . . . In the English department *the ideologies are very different*, and I can't see us ever meeting in the middle – *there is no compromise*.

Another member of the department from the girls' school offered the following observations:

There's one new member of staff . . . – [totalling] six from the old [boys' school], and five from ours – but the five from [the boys' school] are *stronger than us*. There have been some quite unpleasant *clashes of opinion* – before we came to the new school we were told by the new head of department that we would be teaching mixed ability and that it was *not open to discussion*, so any discussion that has tended towards difficulties which people have with teaching mixed ability has been viewed as our failure, rather than our need to have their support and advice.

Several of those involved confirmed that the department had been split down the middle over this issue since the merger. At a departmental meeting which I attended, it was apparent that fiercely opposing views continued to exist on the question, producing an atmosphere of simmering bitterness and resentment, which spilt over at times into open expressions of hostility. Interestingly, at the time of my visits, the policy conflict had been temporarily resolved by an executive decision taken by the headteacher to reintroduce loose ability groupings in the department. This shows that the subordinate discourse in Downland was not totally without influence on matters of policy. Nevertheless, the department continued to be riven by deep ideological divisions at the time of the study, with little sign of a rapprochement between the two camps.

At the eye of the storm in the struggle between the divergent pedagogical discourses in Downland lay disagreements over the nature of provision for students with difficulties in learning. This dispute was personified in the interpersonal conflict between the teaching and learning coordinator and another member of the learning support team, the former special educational needs coordinator of the girls' school; both teachers were also members of the English department, and contributed to the discussion over pupil groupings described above, taking opposing positions (the teaching and learning coordinator in favour of mixed ability teaching, the former special educational needs coordinator for streaming). An English teacher from the former girls' school observed that:

The head of support at that school [that is the former girls' school] has very different ideas from the head of support at this school [that is Downland], and *the two sets of ideas conflict*.

The differences in their points of view about the provision of support for learning have been amply documented in the preceding presentation of the two discourses, and will not be repeated here; however, it is pertinent to adduce further evidence relating to the outcome of the tensions between them. In interview, the former special educational needs coordinator from the girls' school gave vent to powerful feelings of alienation, expressing resentment at what she experienced as the marginalization and undervaluing of her views and expertise:

With the teachers I work with I get very positive feedback, but from the management – [the teaching and learning coordinator] says he values what I do but I'm not convinced, I feel I've rather taken the weight off his shoulders by dealing with statemented students. There was a lot of hassle about that; parents weren't happy. The head, when he gave me the job, said, 'I don't want to end up in court.' That's what I feel about it. I don't think what I am doing is being valued . . . I still feel that *the work I'm doing is not valued because it does approach things from another end.*

A deputy head from the former girls' school offered an account which corroborates the ex-special educational needs coordinator's perceptions:

I think the special needs area, the team there, and a colleague of mine, [the former special educational needs coordinator] – she had enormous scope at [the girls' school] and developed a wonderful programme for those children, but *because the whole thinking was different from here, she has been totally* – she's one of the biggest examples I can think of – *squashed.* She has been desperately trying to push the lid off once in a while and has been *met with total resistance,* but gradually she is beginning to develop and I think that's the way to do it.

From his perspective, the teaching and learning coordinator frankly acknowledged the contradiction between the philosophies of the two previous schools, and the particularly acute tensions among learning support staff since the merger, which (in his view) could lead to deadlock:

As you know, the key to understanding anything at our school is spotting that it's *an uneasy amalgam of two schools with wholly opposite policies and practices. Those philosophies* have not entirely gelled anywhere in the school and are *especially ungelled in our department.* We try to make compromises, and so on, but they don't sit easily together. In fact, I think they *tend to cancel each other out.* In the end, though, it is inevitable that *what I believe will prevail* (because it's cheaper).

Although the tone of the final throwaway comment is tongue-in-cheek, it is noteworthy that these remarks are couched in the language of incompatibility and conflict: there is little sense of the possibility or desirability of a reconciliation between the two opposing philosophies, and the account envisages a resolution of the impasse in terms of the final victory of one approach over the other.

The antagonisms and conflicts found in the English department and over the provision of learning support can be seen as instances of a general phenomenon in the school, namely the dominant influence of staff from the boys' school in defining the ethos of the merged school, and the corresponding marginalization of teachers from the girls' school. A deputy head from the girls' school reflected on the effect on her colleagues:

The more I've seen of this year, the more I tend to feel it's been a *takeover.* It's been sad in a way because I've seen a few of members of staff from [the girls' school] *demoralized.* I know their fields of expertise and I feel they have not been given a chance to really show that, because we've come into a situation where something works well, so we continue it in the [boys' school] style.

Her perceptions were reinforced by the comments of an English teacher from the girls' school, who explained that many ex-girls' school staff had suffered from stress-related illnesses following the merger:

> We've just been expected to come in and *accept all the rules which were given which were the rules of this school previously* . . . quite a lot of us have been unwell, because we just couldn't cope with all the pressures coming from various places.

Quasi-independent corroboration of the view that the merger had in fact amounted to a takeover by the boys' school was provided by an educational psychologist who was employed as a consultant by the school. Commenting on staff morale, she explained that teachers had:

> . . . a lot of grievances to work through of how the whole merger was handled, and it was not handled well. It was very much seen as a [boys' school] *takeover* and a lot of the [girls' school] staff are very aggrieved about a lot of the things. A lot of their positive practices at [the girls' school] have not been absorbed, they've been *ignored*. They have genuine grievances.

A number of institutionalized practices served as indicators to substantiate the interpretation of the merger as a takeover. First was the use of documents from the boys' school as templates for the production of documents for the new, merged school, including: the school brochure (attested by a head of department from the former boys' school); the format of the head's annual report to the governors (reported, and criticized, by a deputy head from the girls' school); and the Teaching and Learning policy document which, as the teaching and learning coordinator acknowledged, was the same document which had been used in the boys' school. Second, a major structural indicator of the takeover was the distribution of posts of responsibility in the new school (see Table 3.1; cf. Ball 1987: 179).

The table demonstrates that a clear majority of senior management and middle management posts in the merged school were occupied by ex-boys' school staff.

Since the majority of girls' school staff were women, and the majority of boys' school staff were men, it is not possible to dissociate the dominance of ex-boys' school staff in the merged school from the subordination of female staff, and from the general question of gender relations in the school. A female English teacher from the girls' school commented:

Table 3.1   Distribution of posts of responsibility in Downland by former school

	Former girls' school	Former boys' school
Senior management	1	3
Heads of department	2	5

There are distinct groupings in the staffroom ... The men who used to work here are incredibly arrogant, and they are the ones who really *denigrate anything that we do*, and a lot of the boys in year 10 have got that.

On the other hand, a woman deputy head (from the girls' school) sought to play down the significance of the 'gender issue', though interspersed in her remarks is evidence of continuing patriarchal assumptions among some male staff, and a certain acceptance of 'macho' behaviour among some boys:

You can talk to people who have been established in the boys' school, like [a subject teacher from the former boys' school] – if he talks about anything, he always talks about boys, and *he has to be reminded there are girls as well*. There are staff who still talk in that vein, and there are staff who remind them not to forget the girls. In terms of the school itself and students, other than *the normal*, sort of, *dominance you get from boys*, I don't think there is a huge gender issue.

A woman teacher of modern foreign languages also remarked upon the distribution of pastoral responsibilities in Downland as a possible sign of stereotyping in the roles assigned to women:

I find it interesting, for want of a better word, that the heads of year 10, 11 and sixth form are men, and that their deputies are women, whereas in year 9 it's a woman who's head and a man who's a deputy ... I think that gives the message very much to year 9 – 'we're being *mothered*'.

Finally, Table 3.2 can be recast to reveal a significant gender imbalance in favour of men in the distribution of posts of responsibility (Table 3.2). The figures for the senior management team include the headteacher, who was, as has been previously noted, a man.

It is also worth remarking that the very language used by teachers from the former girls' school in articulating their feelings of alienation bears unconscious witness to the reality of their subordination as a result of the merger. This can be seen in a number of the comments which were cited above. Their discourse is at times colonized by habits of thinking imposed by the dominant discourse, in phrases such as: 'coming from another school'; the distinction between 'that school' (that is the girls' school) and 'this school' (that is the merged school); the polarization between 'us' and 'this school' implied in '*we've* been expected to accept the rules of *this* school'; and between 'our (previous) situation' and the situation now obtaining which is reflected in

Table 3.2   Distribution of posts of responsibility in Downland by gender

	Women	*Men*
Senior management	2	2
Heads of department	1	6

'*we've come into a situation* where something works well'. In passing comments like these, we can see how the discourse of those marginalized in the merger is powerfully coerced by the perspective of the dominant discourse. Their language enacts the reality of the takeover as a fait accompli at the same time as it protests against it. In a real sense, the struggle to impose a definition of the new, merged school is already conceded in the opposition which can be inferred from these remarks between 'this school' and 'our school'. A similar point might be made about the assumptions about gender roles and relationships embodied in the deputy head's comments about the 'gender issue'. An asymmetry of expectations about the behaviour of male teachers and pupils on the one hand, and female teachers and pupils on the other, is presupposed by the need to remind some staff from the boys' school 'not to forget the girls' – presumably no-one needs to be reminded not to forget the boys. Likewise, to describe dominance by boys as 'normal' presupposes that it is normal for girls to be dominated or retiring. The existence of a gender issue is confirmed at the same time as its significance is minimized.

The evidence shows that the general tenor of the relationships between the divergent pedagogical discourses in Downland School was one of conflict and antagonism. At the time of the study, the discourse of inclusion occupied a position of dominance in shaping the culture of the merged school, whereas the discourse of deviance was in a subordinate position. The recent merger of previously separate girls' and boys' schools had resulted in the marginalization of former girls' school staff, and the repression, in general, of institutional practices and forms of provision associated with the girls' school, in favour of policies followed under the regime of the boys' school. This process of domination and marginalization was reflected in structural indicators such as the distribution of posts of responsibility; in the personal experience of alienation and demoralization expressed by several women from the girls' school consequent upon the amalgamation; and in the unconscious shaping of their discourse, which was invested by the perspective of the dominant discourse at the same time as it protested against it. It is difficult to avoid the conclusion that the merger amounted, in large measure, to an example of the process of 'male takeover' described by (Ball 1987: 200), or, at the very least, to the takeover of the girls' school (whose ethos had been shaped by its mostly female staff) by the boys' school (whose ethos was shaped by its mostly male staff). The outcome was an organizational culture of domination and subordination refracting gender inequalities.

Mediation and the possibility of a complementary relationship

Although the relationship between the discourses of inclusion and of deviance was mainly characterized by conflict and domination, as detailed above, there were glimpses of another possible type of relationship emerging in certain areas. First, at the close of my period of fieldwork in the school, an initiative began aimed at developing provision for able students. This project commanded widespread support, which transcended the boundaries between the constituencies associated with the divergent discourses. For instance, the teaching and learning coordinator, a leading proponent of the discourse of inclusion, welcomed the initiative on the grounds that most teachers perceived provision for the able as a 'problem for the curriculum' rather than a 'problem for the student'; in his view, therefore, the project could act as a vehicle for promulgating the curricular, anti-deficit conceptualization of learning potential which he favoured, and for winning acceptance for this view among a wider section of staff. On the other hand, the former special educational needs coordinator of the girls' school, who was the most prominent proponent of the discourse of deviance, had been an active agitator for the able students initiative, though she held a very different view of its significance. Her philosophy stressed the individual differences between children, and the need for provision to be appropriate to the strengths and weaknesses of each student. For these reasons, she felt that the able students' project was consistent with the aim of developing a continuum of provision, in which the curriculum experienced by some students (whether the most able or those with difficulties) would be different from or additional to that provided for the majority. However, in spite of the opposing rationales advanced within the divergent discourses, the concrete outcome was a working agreement between the different constituencies to collaborate in pursuit of the initiative.

Another example of the possibility of other types of relationship between the two discourses was furnished by the work of the educational psychologist who, as has been mentioned, was employed by the school as a part-time educational consultant. (She did not act in the normal capacity of educational psychologist to the school dealing with matters such as referrals for statementing, a role which was fulfilled in the usual way by the local education authority's psychology service.) By her own account, she had been given a roving, open brief by the headteacher under the general remit of staff development. She offered the perspective of a professional with a close working knowledge of the school, but with no great personal investment in the struggle between the divergent pedagogical discourses. Over a number of issues, she found herself acting as a mediator between the competing perspectives. For example, speaking of the differences over provision for students with difficulties in learning, she said:

> Because my brief was so wide, I could actually adopt the role of *diplomat* between these two approaches . . . I even told [the headteacher] at one stage that I could see these two approaches being *complementary* to one another instead of being antagonistic. There was no reason, other than personalities, that they should be one in opposition to another. The two approaches should surely be complementary . . . I think I still see that as a goal.

As these comments indicate, in her view, the potential existed for the divergent discourses to stand in a reciprocally supportive relationship towards one another, rather than in a relationship of conflict and domination; though this relationship is envisaged as a hypothetical possibility, rather than describing the existing state of affairs in the school. There had, however, been other isolated developments where a degree of compromise or convergence between the two perspectives had occurred. For example, the consultant psychologist described how, initially, the teaching and learning coordinator had refused to allow pupils with statements of special educational need to be withdrawn from mainstream lessons under any circumstances, whereas the former special educational needs coordinator from the girls' school had pressed for greater flexibility over this, in part because she felt that some withdrawal was necessary to make the provision specified in the statements. The psychologist had supported her in this, and, after a period of debate, the teaching and learning coordinator had conceded that a more flexible approach might be adopted, in which withdrawal would sometimes be used. The psychologist argued, reflecting on this debate:

> It's not a matter of principle where things happen, whether it happens in the classroom or outside, that shouldn't be a point of principle, it's what happens. If that pupil is getting a differentiated task or something to build up his skills, it shouldn't be a point of principle where that happens. *There has certainly been some movement on that* in that it's now a much more relaxed approach. It isn't an either/or in that *we're not putting rules on what must and mustn't happen.*

Similarly, the psychologist described her intervention in the English department. As was noted above, this department had been riven since the merger by an ideological debate between the proponents of mixed ability grouping, on the one hand, and streaming, on the other. The consultant had negotiated access to the department on the basis that she would not take sides in the mixed ability–streaming debate, but would offer some feedback on the approaches to differentiation being used in the department. She observed lessons taught by most of the members of the department, then made a report to a departmental meeting describing the various differentiation practices she had seen, along with others she had seen used in other areas of the curriculum – 'a list without any value judgements on'. Whilst the divisions within the department over pupil grouping policy persisted, she felt that her intervention had been of some service in introducing other issues into the debate:

> You could see the polarization and I see myself as a *facilitator of progress*. It's not just the consultation on that issue, it's actually – the subtext – to move this polarized group on.

She felt that her success in mediating between the divergent discourses was due to her position as a relatively detached observer who was not a member of the competing constituencies in the school:

> I have managed to maintain the position as neutral outsider. I am not seen as a member of staff, nor even as a part of the school . . . I've certainly maintained it all the way through and emphasize it in whatever subtle ways I can, the neutral outsider commenting on your institution.

I will return to the question of the relationships between the divergent pedagogical discourses, and their implications for the process of school development, in Chapter 5. In the next chapter, I present a study of another school, Sealey Cove, where initiatives to develop provision were under way, and which displayed some interesting similarities and differences with the case of Downland.

CHAPTER FOUR

Sealey Cove: pupil ability or the presentation of the curriculum?

Sealey Cove High School is a mixed 13–18 comprehensive school of 1150 pupils, maintained by the Local Education Authority, and situated in the suburbs of a large conurbation in the north-east of England. The surrounding residential area from which most of its pupils are drawn is relatively affluent. The school, which was formerly a grammar school, has an established reputation for high academic attainment, which is borne out by the fact that in the school year preceding my visits, over 60 per cent of pupils aged 15 achieved 5 or more GCSE grades A*–C. There is also a thriving sixth form. The perception among staff (in which all interviewees concurred) is that the school's intake contains a high proportion of academically able pupils. As the head of lower school put it:

> The children in the school are academically of a much higher average standard than you would find in most schools. We're *academically skewed towards the top end*.

This perception was reinforced by the special educational needs coordinator, who observed that over one-third of pupils entered the school (at the age of 13) with a reading age of 14+. As a rough indicator, this might suggest the same proportion of academically able pupils in the school.

At the time of the study, there were approximately 75 staff, many of whom were 'long-stayers'; according to the deputy head:

> Quite a number of them have only ever taught here, from the time when it was a grammar school.

For the coordinator, this combination of circumstances was not without its disadvantages:

> It's considered a very academic school, a good middle class school –

ex-grammar school – a school for high achievers, for children who want to achieve academically. As far as special needs go, that's a huge disadvantage.

This perception was shared by two senior managers in the school, one identifying the problem that 'many staff ... haven't been used to dealing with children who have very real needs'; another mentioning a concern about an ambience of complacency prevailing among both staff and pupils: 'The expectations are not being raised the whole time.'

At the time of the study, the school's special educational needs coordinator had been in post for just two terms. It is important to remember that the initiatives to be described below were at an early stage of development. The coordinator's appointment was perceived by the senior management team as a central plank in a deliberate strategy to develop the school's learning support provision, to move it on from the form of provision which had previously prevailed. As the deputy head with overall responsibility for this area commented:

The previous SENCO was in what you might call a *more traditional role* . . . [The new coordinator] comes to it fresh, with *little in the way of preconceived ideas* – which is what we want.

From accounts given by several interviewees, the following picture of provision before the arrival of the new coordinator can be reconstructed. Provision for pupils with special needs was made predominantly through in-class support, often provided by the former special educational needs coordinator herself, and supplemented by some withdrawal of the most vulnerable pupils, for example for an intensive course on comprehension skills. Formally, special needs was treated as a department, analogous to the school's subject departments; and the special educational needs coordinator occupied a position in the school's staffing structure which was on a par with the heads of subject departments. This pattern of provision is broadly consistent with the 'whole school approach' to special needs advocated by many commentators from the mid-1980s onwards, and recommended in several influential pieces of official guidance around the turn of the decade (DES 1989, 1990).

Another indication of the transitional nature of the period when the study was conducted was afforded by the status attributed to the school's current Special Educational Needs policy document by a member of the senior management team, who stressed that it should be seen as out of date. In fact, the policy had been rewritten by the previous special educational needs coordinator in 1994 to take account of the Code of Practice, but according to the deputy head, 'The thinking in the school has moved on since the SEN [Special Educational Needs] policy was written.' Finally, it is not possible to isolate the organization of provision for pupils with difficulties in learning from the general question of pupil grouping arrangements in the school. In this context, a member of the senior management team explained that pupil grouping arrangements – the use of setting, mixed ability groups and so on – varied from one curriculum area to another. At the time of the study, the predominant practice was for pupils to be allocated to sets on the basis of academic information supplied by feeder schools; this had been the established pattern for some years. The practice was under review, however, and the English department had recently taken a decision to move to mixed ability groupings in year 9. The deputy head viewed this as 'a huge step in the right direction'; in her view, the new coordinator, who was a member of the English department, had played a major part in bringing about this change of policy.

In summary, it is suggested that a major reorganization of learning support provision in Sealey Cove was under way at the time of the study. For key members of staff, including the new coordinator and members of the senior management team, it was intended that this should lead to a very different form of provision being adopted throughout the school from the model which had previously prevailed. These interviewees constructed a narrative of the school which defined the past history of special needs provision as less than fully adequate, and embodied a vision of its future articulated in terms of a radical contrast with that past. Further evidence of the form of this narrative will be provided below. For several key figures, it was clear that these initiatives were intended to induce a major reform of practice throughout the school as a whole. My analysis will suggest that (as in the case of Downland reported in Chapter 3) it was possible to discern two discourses of pedagogy in use among teachers in Sealey Cove, corresponding to the discourses of inclusion and deviance (see also Chapter 5). However, the different situational context in Sealey Cove gave rise to a qualitatively different pattern of relationships between the constituencies of staff associated with each discourse. I will describe these relationships in greater detail in the final part of this chapter, but for the present it will be useful to note that there was less evidence of open conflict between the two perspectives in Sealey Cove at the time of the study, and in some areas a working compromise had been forged in support of specific practical initiatives. Significant differences of principle nevertheless remained between the groups of staff concerned, and there was a sense of jockeying for position between rival, and ultimately incompatible, visions of the future development of the school, though no decisive encounter between them had yet taken place. Notwithstanding the revisions of Government guidance and policy which have taken place since the fieldwork was conducted, my experience of using this case study in courses of professional development suggests that conditions in schools remain similar enough for teachers today to identify with the issues raised in the case of Sealey Cove. Other research supports the view that pragmatic developments at school level, such as those discussed here, can be significant in the development of inclusive forms of provision, since the impact of different layers of national education policy is mediated by local circumstances (Thomas and Loxley 2001). Further discussion of the historical roots and continuing relevance of the discourse of deviance and the discourse of inclusion can be found in Chapter 5.

The discourse of inclusion in Sealey Cove: the presentation of the curriculum

In interview, the new coordinator instanced five significant development initiatives with whole school implications in which she was playing a leading role at the time of the study (over and above her statutory responsibilities as the school's special educational needs coordinator). These were: developing provision for able pupils; organizing a 'differentiation team'; carrying out a programme to enhance the reading of pupils with reading difficulties; setting up a scheme to reward pupils' efforts and achievements; and developing equal opportunities policy, including provision for pupils with English as a second language. I will present evidence below relating to each of these initiatives, and interpret their thematic significance for the discourse of inclusion; in addition, evidence of the thinking of other members of staff, some of whom were not directly involved in these initiatives, will be discussed, in an attempt to gauge the base which existed for the reception of the new ideas about support for learning which the coordinator and supporting colleagues were concerned to introduce.

I noted above that the school's intake contained a large proportion of pupils of high academic ability. This seems to have been a consideration in the job description drawn up for the new coordinator's position by the senior management team, which specifically incorporates provision for able pupils as an area of responsibility. It was also, however, an area that the new coordinator had identified herself as a priority for development. As she explained:

> [Provision for able children] was *on my brief* when I was employed here; I immediately recognized that it was an area that was *not catered for* in the school. It's a high achieving school, academically, yet it just seems to happen, it's never been considered overtly. There's no policy for able children, the SEN policy doesn't consider them at all . . . It is a *glaring need* in the school.

As a first step in stimulating the development of provision to meet this need, the coordinator was conducting a review of current provision by collating written information from all subject departments about the strategies which they were already using with more able students.

In collaboration with the head of lower school, she was also liaising with the headteachers of feeder middle schools to revise the information about pupils provided upon transfer to Sealey Cove. In addition to the information normally provided about children with special needs such as medical needs, learning difficulties and statements, feeder schools had been asked to identify pupils with particular talents and abilities. In the first instance, during the year when the study took place, this process of information-gathering and identification had taken place informally ('by word of mouth'), but the system was to be formalized by asking for written information on these pupils in the next intake. The coordinator was also planning to introduce a different system of pupil testing on entry to Sealey Cove, using reasoning tests published by the National Foundation for Educational Research. Amongst other things, she hoped that this would enable the school to identify 'children who have real potential, who are in the top 5 and 10 per cent.' The information thus gathered by the coordinator identifying children with particular talents and abilities was to be disseminated to all staff in the same way and at the same time as information about children with difficulties in learning. As she explained:

[I]t's going to go *all in the same place* – medical information, children with special learning needs, and children with special needs because they're very able, have a particular skill or are not being challenged.

Because of the large number of able pupils in the school, the coordinator saw this as an issue which would by definition have whole school ramifications. In passing, it is worth noting how the coordinator conceptualized the extension of her role to encompass able pupils. She stressed that it was not for her a matter of enlarging the group of pupils for whom she was responsible, but that she saw the thrust on developing provision for the able as part of a multi-faceted strategy to enhance the individualization of learning for all:

I'm not interested in having two sets of people who I'm responsible for – the able and the ones who have difficulties – it's just a *two-edged fork towards differentiation*, and *teaching and learning for the individual*.

A second initiative in which the new coordinator was playing a leading part was the establishment of a learning support working group, also referred to as the 'differentiation team' or team of special needs 'link' teachers. The membership of this team had been identified, and an initial meeting had been held to identify the training needs of team members. It consisted of eight staff, one from each of the major subject departments. Its role was described by the coordinator in the following terms:

The specific brief of that group of teachers is to work with departments *at the planning stage in terms of differentiation*, learning strategies, teaching styles . . . What we want is for the specialism to stay very much within the department but then for us [the differentiation team] to become *specialists in terms of strategies* and ideas, for us to be flexible, offer support, practical possibilities . . . We're not aiming to become subject specialists across the curriculum, but to work very closely with those subject specialists.

Elaborating on her conception of the support role, she described a discussion which had taken place within the senior management team about support teaching in the classroom, which centred on the question of whether subject specialists were needed to provide in-class support in those circumstances where it continued to be needed. The coordinator's position was unequivocal: she believed that 'it's a different skill' – that is the skill(s) needed to provide effective support for learning were independent of subject-specific expertise. The coordinator elaborated on this description by drawing a contrast with another possible model of special needs provision:

Instead of having this special needs department with a couple of people who are *special needs people*, I want to have a team of people who have got a couple of hours on their timetable given over to special needs, but they're not going to sit in a classroom and listen to the teacher talking . . . Their main thrust is going to be on differentiation with departments at the planning stage, so that really what we're doing is *helping teachers be more effective with individual students.*

The key terms here draw a contrast between, on the one hand, a model of provision which (a) sees provision for special needs as the province of a discrete department with its own form of expertise, comparable to the subject-specific expertise of curricular departments; and (b) accords priority to the direct support of pupils by teachers in the classroom; and, on the other hand, a model of provision which (a) sees the primary responsibility for responding to pupils' difficulties in learning as resting with the subject teachers and their departments; and (b) accords priority to the provision of advice, consultation and assistance to these teachers at the planning stage. It will be recalled that the organization of special needs provision at Sealey Cove prior to the arrival of the new coordinator was described in terms very similar to the model which is unfavourably referred to here; the contrast thus seems to carry an implicit challenge to the *status quo ante* in the school. For the coordinator, the role of staff providing support for learning is no longer to assume direct personal responsibility for teaching pupils with special educational needs, and thereby to remove this responsibility from the shoulders of subject teachers, but to provide assistance (especially at the planning stage) to support subject teachers in responding to the full range of pupil diversity – a responsibility which nevertheless remains ultimately in the hands of those subject teachers.

A further aspect of the shift proposed by the coordinator in the definition of the role of learning support staffing was its connection with an ethic of flexible service provision:

I want it to be really flexible – I want the team to *respond to need.* If there is a particular problem that's arisen, say about behaviour or attitude to the subject, that need can be responded to, but it would be a defined need, with a defined aim.

This suggests a modus operandi for the differentiation team which is quite different in terms of the main location, method and outcome of their work from a model predicated on the centrality of support teaching targeted at individually-identified pupils in the classroom:

It's going to be looking at *building up banks of resources with departments,* so departments and special needs people [will be] working closely together . . . It will involve special needs people going into classrooms to assess the children . . . but it will also involve *coming away, writing up ideas, classroom strategies,* resources and so on.

In this account, there is an implicit contrast between a view of special needs staff as dealing with a more or less constant, recurring fraction of the pupil population who persistently present problems (what has been called the 'ambulance service' view of special needs provision (Golby and Gulliver

1979)), and a model which places the reform of curriculum and pedagogy at the heart of its role – a model, in fact, which would make responding to pupils' difficulties in learning an integral part of the school's dynamic of development.

The deputy head with oversight of learning support endorsed the coordinator's view that this activity should not be equated exclusively with in-class support teaching, drawing a contrast between the new coordinator's conceptualization of her role, and the previous model of practice followed in the school:

> The previous SENCO spent most of her time giving in-class support. [The current coordinator]'s less keen on that as an approach. We go along with that, on the grounds that we haven't got a great deal of evidence to suggest that the in-class support that we had before was terribly effective.

The same member of the senior management team substantially corroborated the coordinator's account of the rationale behind the establishment of the differentiation team, noting the disparity between the way of working proposed for this team and a form of provision based on direct support provided by a member of staff with 'specialist' expertise:

> [The special educational needs coordinator] has started to work with representatives of departments. We want to build up a small *team of staff* who will work closely with her, and who will be trained to then go into departments – *trained in differentiating work*, in in-class support . . . We cannot make any real progress with only one SEN specialist in the school doing all the support . . . Budgetary considerations ensure that we will be limited to only that one specialist.

Further support for this perspective was offered by the head of lower school, with whom the coordinator was working closely (see the account of the rewards scheme below):

> For one person to do hands-on in classrooms with staff is practically impossible. [The coordinator]'s idea of developing a team who would (a) increase their skills; (b) speak for those skills in departmental meetings; and (c) a team that could alter in its composition over the years – it seems to me that this is an excellent way forward . . . It's not an alternative; for me, it's the best solution. It is the only way forward, and not just because of financial and staffing constraints, but because *teachers have to be open to the idea of developing skills*, instead of trying to drive the modern child into having the same skills as the teacher . . . There has been a change in education, and we've got to move with society.

It can be seen that two slightly different, but not incompatible, rationales are offered here for the creation of the differentiation team, and the new approach to learning support provision which it embodies. One begins from the constraints imposed by financial considerations, which prevent the employment of more than one special needs 'specialist', and therefore require the wider dissemination of support skills among existing staff; the second acknowledges the existence of these constraints, but attaches priority to the professional development of teachers which it is hoped will ensue from the new form of provision, seeing it as the optimal solution for educational reasons. However, although these accounts differ somewhat in emphasis, it is clear that in practice they converge in supporting the formation of the differentiation team, and the shift in the model of learning support provision which it manifests, a model which places much greater emphasis on support for curriculum development at the planning stage, and correspondingly less emphasis on the provision of in-class support teaching; and which contends that responding to pupils' difficulties in learning is not a 'specialism' on a par with subject specialisms, but is an integral part of teachers' pedagogical expertise, and is therefore an activity which should permeate the school's organizational configuration. This account of the rationale behind the creation of the differentiation team also carries broader implications for the continuing professional development of the staff as a whole, which is seen as central to enhancing the quality of learning for all the school's pupils. This position was epitomized in the comment of a head of year, who was not directly involved in the work of the differentiation team, but was broadly sympathetic to the new perspective embodied in its formation, when she said:

> Staff do have to be able to admit that they need to train without feeling that somehow or other they're saying that they're not good teachers. I think the reverse is true, that *if someone sees the need to change, then they are a good teacher.*

I have documented the strong emphasis placed in the discourse of inclusion on the importance of teachers' professional development, and on the need for flexibility in the choice of teaching methods. The question then arises as to what kind of base existed within the school for the reception of these ideas amongst the majority of teachers who were *not* directly involved in the work of the differentiation team, or in the other cross-curricular initiatives being led by the new coordinator. Was usage of the new discourse about pedagogy confined to a narrow, self-selected group of 'hero innovators'? Or were there other staff whose conceptions of their own practice was in harmony with the principles of the new discourse of pedagogy? I will now review evidence of the range of teaching methods referred to by some other subject teachers in describing their own practice with regard to pupils with varying aptitudes and learning needs, and will attempt to uncover the conceptualization of pedagogy implicit in their accounts.

One teacher of French distinguished between teaching for the 'norm', and recognizing the range of ability in any class: 'you have children on either side [of the norm]'. Elaborating on this, she described some of the strategies she used in teaching French to less able pupils, including: making the lesson more 'practical', for example by asking them to make resources such as flashcards; emphasizing speaking rather than writing; partnering the less able with more able pupils; using more positive reinforcement and praise to raise self-esteem; and giving them a sense that they have a right to speak French. It is clear that this teacher had internalized a sense of personal responsibility for adapting her classroom practice to respond to the diversity of pupil aptitude, and had developed a repertoire of strategies which she was able to draw on in teaching students who experienced difficulties in her subject area. Another teacher, a member of the English department, described her use of different grouping arrangements within the class as part of a flexible approach to enable the participation of pupils of varying levels of ability. She often allowed pupils to work in friendship groups, and found that the groups so formed were generally of mixed ability; but she would also sometimes 'stir it deliberately so that they're in these mixed groups'. She also described strategies for differentiating curricular materials and learning tasks according to pupil ability:

> I might structure the tasks so that the most able are getting extension tasks, and the least able had got a more structured worksheet or task or assignment title. But,

she added,

> I disapprove of preventing a less able child *choosing a task* that was aimed at somebody else; if it was at all feasible, they could have a go at it.

The qualification is important in suggesting a flexible teaching style which allowed a measure of pupil autonomy in the selection of learning activities. This teacher also foresaw a shift in her teaching style in the coming academic year. It will be recalled that the English department had taken a decision to move to wholly mixed ability groupings in the next school year. This member of the department explained how she planned to vary the balance of teaching methods she used in response to this new situation:

> I would expect there to be more occasions on which, having set something up, children are working in groups or individually, and I am going round to support myself . . . because I don't see that given a complete mixed ability set an awful lot of class teaching is going to be effective . . . [But] I still would give stimulus and discussion together, and the group work would follow or precede that.

This account suggests an awareness of the need to adapt pedagogy to suit the changed pupil grouping arrangements; it also expresses a confidence in her ability to respond to the new demand mainly by drawing on strategies which were within her existing repertoire (rather than needing to develop a completely new set of skills). This is consistent with the position found in some recent writing about the teaching of pupils with difficulties in learning, which argues that teachers can accomplish much in responding to a broader range of pupil diversity by employing skills which they already possess, but blending them in a different way and shifting the emphasis placed on different components of their repertoire, rather than having to learn a whole new 'technology of teaching' (compare Clark et al. 1997). It is also consistent with the view of learning support put forward by the coordinator and others leading the reform of provision in the school, which conceptualized the task essentially in terms of curricular and pedagogical development, as opposed to a discrete area of provision distinct from the task of subject teaching. In addition to drawing on a range of methods within the classroom, this interviewee also described a number of ways in which she gave 'extra-curricular' support to the most able and least able pupils, including particularly individual help with spelling and comprehension outside lessons, commenting: 'I would expect as part of my professional duties that I'm delivering the curriculum not just in lesson time.' This provides evidence of a sense of professional commitment and responsibility for pupils' learning which found expression in a pedagogical practice which extended beyond the constraints imposed by the conventional time-tabling of the curriculum.

A final insight into personal teaching style was provided by a teacher of science, who described her own preferred approach in the following terms:

> I try to get all the children excited about the subject of the lesson, and I am conscious that every opportunity I get I will try to stretch them to take further concepts on board. I very rarely tell children anything; I *question*, I *pose hypotheses*.

This suggests a conscious attempt to develop a practice which casts the teacher in the role of extender and challenger of pupils' thinking, in contrast to a didactic model in which the teacher acts as the purveyor of existing knowledge. The teacher aims to stimulate pupils' interest in science, and to provide a model of scientific reasoning through her use of language in the classroom. (It would seem that she was successful in stimulating the interest of at least some of her pupils, since, during the study, she was entered by them in a competition organized by the BBC to find the country's 'best teacher'.)

I have presented evidence about the range of methods referred to by a number of subject teachers in describing their own classroom practice. The specific methods mentioned by the teachers are not particularly novel or unusual in themselves; indeed, many have a long pedigree in the literature on teaching methods for pupils with special educational needs (the importance of positive reinforcement in the teaching of less able pupils, for example, has long been recognized). Rather what these accounts illustrate is a heightened awareness among a section of classroom teachers of the range of methods at their disposal, and a recognition of their responsibility as practitioners to vary the selection of methods which they put into use in response to the varying needs of pupils in their classes. It cannot perhaps be claimed that the methods are fully 'individualized' in the sense of being tailored to the learning styles of every individual pupil; all the teachers interviewed were painfully aware of the reality of constraints imposed by the practicalities of class size and staffing limits. However, their comments do demonstrate a well-developed sense of the range of pupil diversity within any class, and of the need for the class teacher to show flexibility in their teaching style in response to that diversity. The evidence therefore points to the presence in the school of a constituency of established subject teachers in a range of curriculum areas, who shared a conceptualization of pedagogy which was congruent with the curriculum development/professional development model of support for learning which was put forward by the coordinator. These staff articulated a view of themselves as teachers which justifies them being described as self-developing professionals, and recognized their responsibility to play an active part in achieving institutional improvement through the development of their own practice. The presence of a cadre of staff with such a supportive outlook constitutes a favourable condition for the reform of pedagogical thinking and institutional practice which the coordinator and her co-workers were seeking to inspire across the school.

In the case of another initiative led by the coordinator, a programme of intensive support for pupils with difficulties in reading, evidence was already to be found at the time of the study that the scheme had had a cross-curricular impact. In interview, the new coordinator said that, as soon as she arrived in the school, she had identified reading as an issue that needed to have its profile raised. In her view, there were a lot of pupils with reading ages which were surprisingly low for such an academic school. She had a distinctive view of how this issue was to be addressed, however, defined in contradistinction to one approach to the remedial teaching of reading with a long pedigree in special needs practice:

> I didn't want it to be teaching phonetics . . . I wanted just the sheer pleasure of having some nice books . . . It was as much to do with *raising confidence* as to do with raising reading comprehension ages.

The influence of the coordinator's professional background as an English teacher may be detected here, with its tradition of seeing literacy in holistic terms, and an emphasis upon encouraging a love of literature and reading as an inherently rewarding activity, in contrast to a 'basic skills' model of the teaching of reading which was for a long time the dominant tradition in remedial work, which tends to emphasize the direct teaching and reinforcement of sub-skills involved in the development of literacy (such as phonic awareness).

The following account of the reading programme at Sealey Cove is based on information offered by the special needs coordinator in interview, corroborating information given by other interviewees, and related documentary materials. As a target group for intensive intervention, the 12 pupils with the lowest reading ages in the school were identified; all had reading ages below 10 years. These pupils were withdrawn from the mainstream curriculum and taught by the coordinator and another supporting teacher in two groups of six, for one hour per day over a period of six weeks (a total of 30 hours' direct tuition). During these sessions, the pupils' activity was given over to the practice of reading for pleasure, with support and encouragement from the coordinator and her assistant. The coordinator's classroom and office base, where these sessions took place, was resourced with a generous collection of reading books chosen by the coordinator herself. The majority of these were fiction (short novels and anthologies of stories) aimed at teenagers; the coordinator had tried to ensure that their content and appeal was age-appropriate, that is that they would not be perceived as 'babyish' by the pupils. Pupils were encouraged to choose reading texts according to their interests, but might be guided by the coordinator if she thought it necessary. In order to evaluate the effects of the reading programme, the coordinator recorded pre- and post-test data which showed a general significant improvement in the reading and comprehension ages of the pupils as measured by standardized tests. She reported these results to a meeting of heads of department, where the success of the programme was acknowledged and produced a positive response. Heads of department, including some who had initially been resistant to the programme, commented that they and their staff had noticed an improvement in the pupils' attitudes to themselves and to their schoolwork, manifested in improvements in behaviour and concentration in the classroom. They also began to put forward their own proposals for raising the profile of reading in the school, making suggestions for example for improvements in the school library, and the possibility of setting up a 'bookswap' scheme.

This account of the scheme's development and impact was substantially corroborated by a member of the senior management team:

> [The special educational needs coordinator] came up with the idea [of the reading programme] and we decided that we wanted to try it. There was quite a lot of suspicion from heads of department; some of them initially were quite antagonistic towards the idea. . . . The reading ages of the children who were involved in the small groups went up. As a result of that, the heads of department were very supportive of the suggestion that we try it again . . . The things that were said were not so much about the reading of the children, but more about their confidence and their attitude. People had actually noticed *a difference in their confidence and their attitude in the classroom* in a very short time.

As in the case of the coordinator's comments, it is noteworthy that the justificatory rationale retrospectively advanced here in accounting for the success of the reading programme emphasizes the perceived beneficial effects upon pupils' self-esteem and self-concept as learners, rather than measurable gains in reading scores, or the remediation of deficits in basic literacy skills per se. The reading programme, an apparently bounded and self-contained initiative, was also placed in an organizational development perspective by the coordinator, demonstrating her capacity for strategic thinking. First, she saw it as an example of an initiative whose success was widely acknowledged among staff, thereby helping to create a favourable climate towards further innovations in strategies for supporting the learning of pupils with difficulties. Second, she saw it as part of the drive to encourage subject departments and teachers to accept primary responsibility for addressing pupils' learning difficulties, saying that 'after this big push' in the first year, 'the responsibility needs to pass back' to subject departments. This plan seemed to be on course, since, with the support of heads of department, an expansion of the reading support programme was planned for the following academic year, which would involve a wider section of staff in supporting the reading of a larger group of pupils.

A further whole school development initiative in which the coordinator was playing a leading role was a project to set up a system of rewarding pupils for their efforts and achievements. As in the cases of provision for able pupils and support for reading, the coordinator had herself identified this as a lacuna in the school's existing provision, as viewed through the lens of her personal conceptualization of how difficulties in learning arise, and her broader pedagogical philosophy:

> The other issue that was glaring was there's no rewards system, and I don't believe in having a discipline system without a rewards system . . . I see it as a way to *differentiate and encourage*, and very much *part and parcel of special needs*, especially if you reward for a range of things – you reward a lot of kids . . . I'm very much a believer in *positive discipline* – pick out what they can do and concentrate on that, and reward them for it.

However, she also saw it as a local developmental need arising from the character of the school's intake, containing as it did a high proportion of pupils with talents and abilities who were likely to succeed in their schooling:

> I think the school would benefit [from a reward system] because we've got so many kids that we can reward – I don't know why we're not telling them how wonderful they are all the time.

At the time of my visits to the school, the coordinator had begun work on this project with the head of lower school. They were collaborating on developing the concept and on taking the first steps towards information-gathering and trialling. Together they had devised a simple questionnaire which was shortly to be used at an evening meeting with the parents of the forthcoming intake of pupils, asking parents to identify their child's skills and talents, their views on what efforts and achievements the school should reward, and how the school should reward these. Through this means, the coordinator and her collaborator were beginning to seek ways of involving parents in their child's education, and improving and developing communications between school and parents. The coordinator also described how she saw the rewards system being developed from this beginning, demonstrating a tactical sense of how a change in school policy such as this might be implemented. She envisaged the formation of a working party consisting of herself, the head of lower school, representatives of the heads of departments and heads of year:

> . . . and a couple of others who are *willing to put in some graft* and are interested – so a very small group of teachers who actually get everything together, and make sure that it links in with the discipline policy.

It was also planned that the system would be introduced only with year 9 pupils in the first instance, so that staff would have a 'limited clientele' at first; it would then be spread up the school if the scheme proved successful. The desired change in school-wide practice would thus be phased in gradually. The coordinator recognized that, if the scheme was to have a genuine impact on practice, it would need to command the support of both heads of department and heads of year, and planned to involve representatives of both groups at an early stage in its development. The project, however, established a particularly close link between learning support provision and pastoral provision in the school, marking a direct attempt to shift the ethos of the prevailing approach to pupil discipline and behaviour across the whole school.

If successful, this initiative would have wide-ranging ramifications for the school at a deep cultural level; the first steps were being taken to pave the way for a wider shift of policy and practice in the future.

A final area of whole school development which the new coordinator had taken on board was the question of equal opportunities policy, and in particular its connection with provision for pupils with English as a second language. At the time of my fieldwork visits, developments in this field were at an early stage. The coordinator had begun to assist a colleague in exploring how policy and provision in this area, which had previously been underdeveloped in the school, could be improved. As the coordinator remarked:

> There's not a policy in this school yet [for equal opportunities] or a development plan, but it's very high on the head's list of priorities . . . At the moment the issue is children who have English as a second language.

The coordinator had contacted the LEA officer responsible for provision for pupils with English as a second language, who was due to come into the school in the following term with a specific brief to investigate staying-on rates and home-school liaison for this group of pupils. The number of pupils concerned was thought to be small, estimated to be about eight or nine in total by the coordinator; but as she pointed out, 'we don't really know.' For the coordinator there was a clear link between the attitude to bilingual pupils and the wider question of the school's orientation to equal opportunities issues, and also to the valuing of the diverse range of students' talents and abilities. Speaking about bilingualism amongst the pupils, she said:

> I think it's kept under wraps and I want to *celebrate it* and change the attitude to it.

As a specific target, she planned in the next academic year to ensure that the school would make provision for bilingual pupils to take an examination in their home language. She also anticipated that the revision of the school's policy on special educational needs would incorporate reference to the principles of equality of opportunity and equal valuing of all pupils, regardless of ability, and to the need to recognize and celebrate the manifold talents which pupils bring to school.

From the preceding account of the five initiatives of whole school significance in which the coordinator was playing a leading part, it will be clear that she had adopted a broad interpretation of her remit, which was centrally concerned with stimulating curricular and pedagogical development across the school, rather than narrowly defined in terms of supporting a small group of pupils with particular difficulties in learning. It is therefore important to assess what personal and professional qualities she possessed which might equip her to undertake such a leadership role, oriented towards making organizational change happen. I will now review evidence relating to the special educational needs coordinator's leadership capabilities.

The coordinator's professional background was 'non-traditional' in the sense that she had previously been the head of the English department in a secondary school, that is she had not previously been a 'special needs specialist' before taking up her new position. She was not without relevant professional development, having previously done an Open University course in special educational needs. However, in her own words, her English background was very important in shaping her view of the learning support task: 'I bring my English background to the job, and it taints everything I do.' It will be noted that this unconventional background and perspective is compatible with the qualities sought by the school's senior management, as mentioned above (that the new coordinator should 'come to it fresh,' with few 'preconceived ideas'). Its influence could also be detected in the coordinator's attitude towards promoting literacy in pupils with reading difficulties, which was described above.

Amongst the positive professional qualities which the coordinator displayed was what might be termed a sense of 'strategy and tactics' in relation to the pursuit of school development initiatives. For example, in interview the coordinator articulated her own primary goal as follows:

> I want to move it [that is provision for supporting student's learning] on again, dragging most of the staff behind me. My *major aim over the next 12 months is to move away from special needs as a department to special needs as a whole school thing*; and it's got the full backing of the head and the senior management. It's quite a big change of direction, and it's quite difficult to pin down exactly how we're going to work until we've tried it.

In this account, the coordinator provides evidence of: her willingness to assume personal responsibility for leadership; the ability to articulate the primary organizational development priority which she perceived for the year ahead; an awareness of the importance of senior management support in realizing this objective; and a recognition of the significance of this priority for the school as a whole ('a big change of direction'). Taken together, these factors show a well-developed strategic sensibility on her part, and the ability to articulate a whole school perspective which transcends the purview of the individual class teacher or the particularistic concerns of the subject department. In conjunction with this strategic sensibility, the coordinator also demonstrated what might be termed a tactical awareness:

> I'm trying to *lower my profile* a bit, because I need people not to see me as a threat, or that I'm into power, which I'm not . . . It would be absolutely *impossible to function if you were part of any staffroom clique* . . . It's vital that you have a lot of one-to-one contact with all members of staff – my team needs to be everybody.

Here the coordinator shows an awareness of the need to adjust her self-presentation to other staff in order to avoid being perceived as a threat. There is a sense of the need to pace herself and to stand back and consolidate at times if this is necessary in pursuit of the overriding goal of whole school reform.

A third element of her leadership capabilities was what might be termed an 'opportunistic' orientation towards externally-mandated change. Many commentators have remarked unfavourably on the bureaucracy and paperwork introduced by the Code of Practice (which laid out in fine detail a revision of the procedures associated with the identification of pupils with special educational needs (DFE 1994a)), especially in the requirement for Individual Education Plans (IEPs) for all students at Stage 2 or above in the assessment process (for example Hart 1996). This may be perceived as a particular problem in large secondary schools, where, for each pupil causing concern, all relevant subject teachers are expected to contribute to the drawing up of an IEP and to be involved in its regular revision and updating – a major administrative task in such a school. In Sealey Cove, the coordinator's attitude was rather more ambivalent:

> Some of the rigidity that the Code of Practice forces is a pain, but if you do have everything in situ, then *people do take you seriously*, which is OK.

In particular, she believed that IEPs had raised awareness among staff about children with non-statemented special educational needs. She felt that this outcome was beneficial and 'worth the paperwork'. This example shows how she was able to recognize some positive benefits in externally-mandated changes in procedure which many teachers have viewed in an entirely negative light.

Finally, the coordinator showed that she was able to make a realistic assessment of her own position in relation to the rest of the staff in the school:

> Some of them are very *sympathetic*, some of them are naturally *antagonistic* because of their moral and political viewpoint, some people just *despise change* . . . and a lot of staff, because I'm new, *still haven't got a clue where they stand*.

This tripartite division into supporters of change, resistors and neutrals echoes similar distinctions often made in the school organization literature (Ball 1987). More significantly for the present purpose, it reveals that the coordinator was able to maintain a positive commitment to the challenge of leading school change without succumbing to a 'rose-tinted' view of the organizational and interpersonal context in which she found herself.

I have presented evidence to demonstrate that the coordinator was able to bring to bear the following qualities in interpreting her role: a strategic sensibility; tactical awareness; an opportunistic orientation towards externally-mandated change; and the ability to make a realistic assessment of her own position within the context of the range of attitudes of the staff who make up the organization. Taken together, these qualities provide evidence of well-developed capabilities to stimulate and guide school-wide change. Comments made by a member of the school's senior management team show that the coordinator's thinking with regard to the development of provision was in keeping with those in the school with executive responsibility for whole school issues, both in terms of the specific goals she identified, and the manner of their realization:

> We want to see *responsibility for meeting the needs of all students taken on by the departments themselves*. . . . Departments have varied: some departments have taken on the challenge of differentiating the work that they present to the children very well; but there are still other departments who

see *special needs as somebody else's responsibility* . . . We'll *concentrate our efforts* in a couple of departments rather than trying to spread ourselves too thinly [in the first year] – departments which have already suggested that they'd really like to be involved . . . [special needs provision] varies very much from one department to another. It becomes obvious often because of the number of discipline problems . . . I would hope that by the end of 12 months, we could see two or three departments feeling much *more confident about their ability to deal with special needs* . . . I think we probably need to concentrate our efforts in a few departments to start with, and then move on from there.

Embodied in these comments is an evaluation of the current state of provision which is consistent with that made by the coordinator, though perhaps placing a more pointed emphasis on the perceived shortcomings of some subject departments as they stand at present. The strategic priority for development which the deputy head identifies on the basis of this critique is, in any case, very much one shared with the coordinator: the need for subject departments to take on primary responsibility for responding to the full range of pupil diversity, rather than passing responsibility over to a 'specialist in special needs'. There is also evidence in this account of an understanding of the need for the tactical targeting of effort: thus the thrust for development would be concentrated initially in a small number of departments who were willing to be involved. This echoes the coordinator's sense of the dynamic nature of the change process, in which it might be necessary to shift the focus of one's activity from one area to another at different stages. As in the case of the coordinator's comments, a goal for the year ahead is articulated. The different phrasing of these goals is probably best accounted for by the difference in the organizational perspective of the two staff: for the special educational needs coordinator, the emphasis was on changing the definition and perception of the role of learning support staffing in the school (especially the 'differentiation team'); for the deputy head, the emphasis is placed directly on changing the functioning of subject departments. Nevertheless, both formulations are consistent with the primary goal of shifting responsibility for responding to pupils' difficulties in learning increasingly on to the activities of subject teachers and departments, and away from a view of special needs provision as the responsibility of other staff with specialist expertise; they are, in a sense, two sides of the same coin. Both perspectives are directed towards the overall goal of school improvement reflected ultimately in the enhanced learning of all pupils.

In this section, I have presented evidence to suggest that a common outlook was current among a number of staff in Sealey Cove school with regard to the nature of students' difficulties in learning and the provision which should be made in response to those difficulties. Foremost in articulating this discourse of inclusion was the newly-appointed special educational needs coordinator, though the evidence has shown that a similar perspective was substantially shared by a constituency of staff which spanned members of the senior management team and class teachers from several subject departments. Because of the recent nature of the coordinator's appointment and the associated whole school initiatives which she was leading, it would be premature to claim that this discourse had become entrenched across the school at the time of the study. However, it was clear that the discourse had already made an impact upon cross-curricular provision and practice in several areas; furthermore, in view of the coordinator's leading involvement in the revision of aspects of whole school policy which was under way, and the strong support for her work expressed by senior staff, it seemed likely that the discourse would continue to exercise a significant influence on the direction of the school's development in the medium term. The discourse of inclusion informed these teachers' thinking about teaching and learning along a number of dimensions, which are summarized below:

- The adaptation of pedagogy should be guided by a recognition of each pupil's individual identity as a learner, formed from a unique profile of capabilities and difficulties (rather than being shaped by categorical definitions of pupil identity, for example able vs. 'SEN');
- In the provision of support for learning, priority should be accorded to working with departments to support the differentiation of the curriculum at the planning stage (rather than to the provision of teaching assistance in the classroom);
- Responding to pupils' difficulties in learning should be seen as an integral part of teachers' generic pedagogical expertise (rather than a form of specialist expertise analogous to subject-specific content knowledge);
- Primary responsibility for addressing the full range of learner diversity resides with subject departments (rather than being the province of a discrete special needs department);
- The continuing professional development of the whole teaching staff is central to enhancing the quality of learning experienced by all the school's pupils. (This might be contrasted with a view of the teacher's professional expertise as centring in the possession of a fixed body of content knowledge.);
- Teachers can accomplish much in attuning their teaching to the spectrum of aptitude which exists in any student group by drawing flexibly upon a repertoire of familiar pedagogical methods to modify the classroom learning environment. (The acquisition of a new 'educational technology' is not a prerequisite for teachers to present a curriculum which is more responsive to learner diversity.);
- The justificatory rationale for interventions aimed at improving pupils' core skills (such as reading ability) emphasizes the benefits to the pupil's self-concept as a learner and their confidence to participate in a common mainstream curriculum (rather than placing the emphasis narrowly upon gains in basic skills for their own sake, or the need for an alternative curriculum to be provided on a permanent basis);
- Enhancing the school's capacity to respond to learner diversity requires a shift in organizational culture towards regularly rewarding pupils for their successes in learning (and away from a prevailing conception of discipline framed in terms of punitive sanctions);

- There is a need to recognize and celebrate the manifold talents which pupils bring to schooling by virtue of their diverse cultural backgrounds (as opposed to providing a curriculum predicated upon the assumption of cultural homogeneity);
- The role of the special educational needs coordinator is conceived in terms of promoting the school-wide development of curriculum and pedagogy (rather than in terms of the direct teaching of an identified group of 'SEN' pupils); more generally, the task of supporting pupils' learning is equated with the process of school improvement (rather than with the remediation of the deficits of individual pupils).

The discourse of deviance in Sealey Cove: pupil ability

I have argued that the thinking of a range of teaching staff about students' difficulties in learning was governed by a number of characteristic beliefs; taken together, these can be seen to comprise a discourse of inclusion. There is evidence that this outlook was already exercising an influence on the reshaping of aspects of school policy and forms of provision. This was not the only perspective upon students' difficulties in learning which was to be found among teaching staff in Sealey Cove, however. In what follows, I will illustrate the principal characteristics of a second system of ideas, which corresponds to that which I call the discourse of deviance (see also Chapter 5). The account which follows will draw substantially on evidence relating to the mathematics department, which in Sealey Cove was a stronghold of the discourse of deviance; however, salient material relating to other departments will also be presented, demonstrating that support for this outlook existed among a sub-group of teachers which spanned a range of curriculum areas.

A key point of departure which differentiates the discourse of deviance from the discourse of inclusion lies in its working hypothesis regarding the origin or cause of difficulties in learning. Within the discourse of deviance, the cause of difficulties in learning is seen as the pupil's relative deficit in cognitive ability. For example, the head of the mathematics department explained his department's support for the reading support programme initiated by the new coordinator (which was described above) in the following terms:

> My main concern at the moment isn't the numerical ability of the kids, it's *comprehension* – the reading and understanding ... If we can free people from that, if we can *give them greater skills*, that would help the maths department no end. As a recognition of that, I'm supporting the reading programme that [the special educational needs coordinator]'s doing ... What we lose in maths time, hopefully we'll gain in the end with greater comprehension. .... To get a grade at GCSE ... they've got to understand the words that are being used, so *the solution to me is not to make worksheets simpler to understand, but to improve the child's reading ability and comprehension.*

It will be apparent that the understanding of learning difficulties expressed in these comments differs significantly from that articulated in the discourse of inclusion which I described above. In the present account, the source of the problem is located firmly within the individual pupil, in terms of weaknesses in fundamental aspects of cognition (such as understanding) and in related basic skill areas (such as reading). The account constructs a polarity between pupils' potential ability in mathematics (which is dependent upon an under-lying numerical ability), and their lack of skills in reading comprehension, which is seen as a prerequisite on which the teaching of mathematics should be able to rely. As a corollary, the kind of intervention required in response to these concerns is seen in terms of redressing the child's shortcomings in basic literacy skills. From this perspective, therefore, organizational responsibility for making provision in response to pupils' difficulties in learning lies outwith the subject department; indeed, the idea that the subject teacher should take responsibility for adapting their own teaching materials or methods is explicitly rejected. This position stands diametrically opposed to the discourse of inclusion in terms of: the causal attribution which is made in accounting for students' difficulties in learning; the model of provision which is advocated in response to those difficulties; and the locus of responsibility which is identi-fied for making such provision. (In spite of these major differences in outlook, however, it is worth remarking that the speaker voices support for the particu-lar initiative in question, that is the reading support programme; this point will be elaborated upon below in examining the relationships which were obtained between the two discourses.)

As I illustrated above, one theme of the discourse of inclusion was a predis-position towards the notion of a common curriculum for all pupils. The discourse of deviance, by contrast, advocated the provision of qualitatively different curricula for pupils according to their discrete levels of ability. One example of an alternative form of curriculum provision was furnished by the 'graduated assessment scheme' operated by the mathematics department. The following account of the scheme draws principally on information provided by the head of department and another member of the department who acted as the scheme's coordinator. In essence, the school offered two discrete routes which pupils might follow towards attaining a GCSE qualification in math-ematics. The majority of pupils were entered through the 'mainstream' route, assessed by a terminal examination paper. The graduated assessment scheme provided an alternative route which, in the words of the head of department, was 'originally introduced for children with special educational needs.' The scheme was a variant of a form of provision which was in widespread use in English secondary schools. Pupils following this route worked through pub-lished curriculum materials (workbooks) at their own individual pace (under the supervision, of course, of the class teacher). Whole class teaching was rarely used. Pupils sat modular assessment papers as they progressed through the course, and were awarded certificates in recognition of their positive achievements in these assessments. Whilst it was theoretically possible for pupils following the graduated assessment scheme to gain the full range of GCSE grades, in practice these pupils mainly attained grades in the lower range (below C). In the view of members of the department, the scheme was effective because it offered short-term, attainable goals with rapid rewards. In Sealey Cove, the member of the department who coordinated the scheme was also a member of the 'differentiation team', and fulfilled the role of 'link teacher' between the mathematics department and the special educational needs coordinator. The head of department evaluated the scheme's success in the following terms:

> I think we [that is the Maths Department] pioneered the recognition that there are *kids in the school for whom mainstream GCSE might not be appropriate*, and we investigated and found this scheme which we've used for some considerable time, and which we find to be of proven worth, in terms of the lack of discipline problems that we get within these classes, the enthusiasm that's there, the desire to succeed, the kids coming back after they've left school to get their certificate, attending the final exam rather than just opting out and missing it, and the actual grades that they've achieved. So we're not complacent, but we're very happy about it.

The perceived success of the scheme had led to a rapid increase in the number of pupils following this route. At the time of the study, some 90 pupils were enrolled on the scheme, comprising the bottom three sets in mathematics. The top three sets were following the mainstream GCSE route, though the size of these sets was larger.

The operation of the graduated assessment scheme, and the rationale offered for its use, again indicate the presence in the school of a model of provision for pupils with difficulties in learning which differed substantially from that defined within the discourse of inclusion. The difficulties which the scheme was designed to address are defined in terms of the low academic ability possessed by some pupils, for whom the mainstream curriculum is 'not appropriate', and for whom a discrete, alternative route must be provided. Differentiation in this case takes place through pupil grouping arrangements (setting by ability) and the provision of qualitatively different curricula, rather than through the model indicated in the discourse of inclusion of the subject teacher adapting a common curriculum to the varying needs of learners within a heterogeneous teaching group.

It will be apparent that the question of the provision of alternative curricula cannot be divorced from the organizational issue of pupil grouping arrangements throughout the school. I noted above that a disposition in favour of mixed ability groupings was characteristic of teachers employing the discourse of inclusion. By contrast, a policy of strict setting by ability remained the rule in both the mathematics and modern languages departments. The head of mathematics explained how the size of sets was varied as part of the department's response to the needs of the less able:

> I've got 35 kids in the *top set*; that's the price we pay for having 10 children in the *bottom two sets* . . . – a deliberate policy, not necessarily popular with the hierarchy, but *the only way we can deal with it*; and those 10 kids would probably get a support teacher as well.

Once again, these comments suggest a somewhat different perspective on responding to learner diversity from that found in the discourse of inclusion, and indeed embody an explicit recognition that there is a divergence of perspectives within the school over this issue. Although the cleavage between ideological positions on this issue was recognized to run deep by staff on both sides of the divide, it is important to note that representatives of subject departments with contrasting pupil grouping policies (mathematics and foreign languages on the one hand, and English on the other) were equally anxious to emphasize that all members of their departments taught throughout the age and ability range. No teacher in these departments was designated to teach only the less able (or more able) pupils to the exclusion of others. This gave some grounds for optimism about the possibility in the long term of creating a more widely shared consensus within the school upon provision for the full range of pupil diversity. Notwithstanding their fundamental differences over a range of issues, from within both discursive perspectives all teachers were seen to share responsibility for teaching across the ability range, including the teaching of pupils who were encountering difficulties in learning. It is possible that this shared experience would militate against the entrenchment of the view of provision for difficulties in learning as 'someone else's responsibility' which was mentioned above, and provide a material basis for the favourable reception of the contrasting view of pedagogy encapsulated in the discourse of inclusion.

My analysis of the discourse of inclusion in Sealey Cove suggested that the central place which it accorded to the skills of adapting the curriculum and varying teaching methods entailed that teachers' professional development was also seen as a constant priority in developing the school's provision for pupil diversity. Not all staff shared this view, however. A much more sceptical attitude towards 'INSET' activities was expressed by several members of the science and mathematics departments in particular. In the 18 months before the case study visit, there had been two whole staff training days about differentiation, and, since her arrival, the new coordinator had also led training meetings for colleagues on the topic. Commenting on these formal training events, a member of the mathematics department said:

> It does grate a little when you attend meetings [about differentiation] – I've attended these meetings for 10 years, and I always get the same information passed to me – worksheets have to be clearly typed, whatever . . . People come out with these ridiculous statements all the time, and it's people who've read about it, and have little *practical experience*, or it's been such a long time ago. They think they're being helpful, and it isn't . . . The worksheets, and the approach is always more orientated towards geography, English, history, *wordy subjects* where there's more scope for the sort of approach that they're using. And it grates a little, it's like being at college again . . . [The special educational needs coordinator] has run meetings about SEN during and after school time which I've attended, but I must say *I've heard it all before* – you know, the *theory*.

In these comments, the 'theory' of differentiation (advocated by others) is unfavourably counterposed to the wisdom of 'practical experience' (implicitly ascribed by the speaker to the point of view to which he subscribes); doubt is cast through a number of phrases on the innovative quality of the new approach to support for learning represented by the discourse of inclusion, and advocated in particular by the coordinator; and the generally negative attitude expressed by the speaker towards both the experience of in-service training and the concept of differentiation is reinforced by the notion that he belongs to a subject-specific subculture with its own unique demands which render this approach inappropriate to his disciplinary specialism. It is clear from this evidence, and from similar comments made by other members of the science and mathematics departments, that consensus on the central import- ance of teachers' professional development had not been reached in the school, and indeed that there was some resistance to this perspective on the part of established members of staff in core curriculum areas.

Examination of the discourse of inclusion showed that it embodied a par- ticular conceptualization of 'support' for learning, and the modus operandi of staff involved in its provision. The direct provision of in-class teaching support was de-emphasized, in favour of support for differentiation of the curriculum at the planning stage; furthermore, the task of adapting teaching in response to pupil diversity was seen as a generic aspect of pedagogical expertise, which consequently did not require the possession of specialist subject knowledge on the part of members of staff involved in supporting this process. Another, contrasting view of support teaching and the skills which it required was articulated by the head of mathematics. In interview, he gave an account of how in-class support was organized in practice, and his views on its effectiveness:

> It will certainly never be another maths teacher [who provides in-class support] because we have so few *specialist* maths teachers . . . We have 7, soon to be 6 . . . It's possible that it'll be another member of staff who is likely to have no *specialist knowledge* – it's just that their timetable is not full, so this is what you do. They're of some use, not least because they're more willing to say, 'I don't understand this,' and a kid can relate to that . . . It's an extra body in the class; it simply *avoids a queuing system*, that's all it is . . . There's no targeting; it's whoever's free at the time. It's sporadic and infrequent, and will continue to be, given our staffing problems . . . I'm resigned to it. It's never been the case, and it's a luxury we'll never be able to afford, really, because I'm well aware that what I'm asking for, every other head of department would wish, so you'd probably need to have *ten different special needs people*.

A central organizing concept in this account is the notion of specialist subject knowledge, in this case of mathematics. It is conceded that non-specialists who provide in-class support can be 'of some use'; but permeating the account is an implicit contrast between the teacher with specialist subject knowledge, who would be capable of providing genuine support for learning in the class- room, and the non-specialist whose presence is mainly of assistance in avoid- ing problems of classroom management. Superficially, there might appear to be some overlap between the speaker's concept of 'ten different special needs people' and the formation of the differentiation team being led by the special educational needs coordinator. However, on closer inspection, the logics underlying the two proposals can be seen to contradict one another. The discourse of deviance affirms the view that a teacher's professional expertise depends first and foremost on their possession of specialist subject knowledge; if the teacher possesses this knowledge, then they are better equipped to fulfil the role of providing in-class teaching support for pupils with difficulties in learning. This stands in contrast to the view of the relation between teaching and 'support' work articulated in the discourse of inclusion, according to which the adaptation of the curriculum, and of the teaching methods used in its presentation, should be seen as central to the generic pedagogical expertise which all teachers need to develop; consequently, the task of providing 'support for learning' does not depend primarily on the teacher's possession of specialist subject knowledge for its effectiveness.

In the preceding analysis I have shown the currency in Sealey Cove of a second outlook upon pupils' difficulties in learning and the type of provision which the school should make in response. This perspective corresponded to what I call the discourse of deviance, and diverged systematically from the discourse of inclusion along a series of dimensions. The evidence suggests that the constituency of support for the discourse of deviance was concentrated in particular subject areas, notably mathematics, but that it can justifiably be described as a shared perspective which carried some weight in the institution (finding adherents both among established staff in middle management positions, and class teachers). The discourse tended to be deployed in defence of certain aspects of the existing organization of provision, and as a critique of recent innovations which threatened to upset the prevailing status quo; compared with the discourse of inclusion, there was less evidence of the discourse of deviance contributing positively to the process of revision of school policy which was under way. The principles which characterized the discourse of deviance as it was articulated in Sealey Cove can be summarized as follows.

- The origin or cause of difficulties in learning lies in relative deficits in the cognitive ability of some pupils (rather than in deficiencies in the presentation of the curriculum by teachers);
- Intervention in response to learning difficulties should concentrate upon efforts to remediate the shortcomings of these pupils in basic areas of functioning and performance (rather than upon the reconstruction of the regular curriculum);
- The locus of organizational responsibility for provision for difficulties in learning lies outwith the subject department, that is with an organizationally distinct special needs department (as opposed to the primary responsibility lying with the subject department);
- Discrete, qualitatively different curriculum routes should be provided for pupils according to the stratum of ability to which they belong (as opposed to the provision of a common curriculum for all pupils, the presentation of which is differentiated by the subject teacher); there is a hierarchy of ability and a corresponding stratification of provision;

- The organization of provision is justified as a pragmatic accommodation to necessity (rather than by appeal to positions of value or principle);
- The centrality of specialist subject knowledge possessed by teachers is asserted in defining the nature of their professional expertise (rather than the capacity to vary and adapt their own pedagogical practice);
- The preferred form of support for learning is direct teaching assistance in the classroom (as opposed, for instance, to advice on differentiation of the curriculum at the planning stage);
- The accumulated wisdom of practical experience is the source of legitimation in evaluating the utility of proposals for the reform of teaching methods (rather than educational theory); scepticism is expressed about the value of professional development activities.

Relationships between the divergent pedagogical discourses

In this chapter, I have documented the currency in Sealey Cove of two divergent pedagogical discourses which were associated with different constituencies of teaching staff. The outlook encapsulated in the discourse of inclusion represented a departure from the traditions and patterns of provision which had previously been dominant in the school, a challenge to the organizational *status quo ante*; whereas the discourse of deviance was mobilized in defence of prevailing custom and practice. Neither discourse could be said to occupy an unequivocally dominant position at the time when the study was conducted; however, the discourse of inclusion was positioned to exercise a greater influence on the review of major areas of school policy which was under way. Whilst there was little open conflict between the two perspectives at the time of the study, it will be apparent that the ramifications for the school of one discourse or the other becoming predominant were very different; the two discourses prescribed contrasting trajectories for the future development of the school. In the final part of this chapter, I will analyse the relationships between the discourses in more detail.

Working compromise

In the case of the reading support programme, there was evidence of a successful working agreement being forged between the constituencies associated with the divergent discourses. It will be recalled that the special educational needs coordinator, in justifying this initiative (which she proposed and led), offered a rationale which emphasized the importance of encouraging pupils to value reading as an intrinsically rewarding activity, and the increased confidence and self-esteem displayed by pupils on returning to mainstream lessons. From a contrasting perspective, the head of mathematics expressed support for the scheme as a means of remediating the weak comprehension skills of low ability pupils, rejecting the notion that it should be the responsibility of subject teachers to differentiate the presentation of the mathematics curriculum in response to these pupils' needs. In spite of these contradictory rationales, the net outcome was that the divergent pedagogical discourses at work in Sealey Cove converged in support of this specific practical initiative. Furthermore, the perceived success of the reading support programme had led heads of department who had initially been hostile to the idea to propose their own ideas for developing reading as a cross-curricular issue, indicating that the compromise achieved between the two discourses over this issue had a generative effect in extending pedagogical thinking in the school.

In addition to this example of a compromise in practice between the two discourses, there was evidence of an occasional blurring of the boundaries between them. Whilst the distinctions between them were clear in respect of their orientation towards existing patterns of provision, there was some evidence of an overlap between the discourses when it came to the theoretical understanding of the term 'special educational needs' held by teachers. The majority of interviewees who offered a definition of the term referred to the notion of a 'continuum' of ability, explicitly extending the application of the term 'special needs' to embrace both the most able and the least able students. The following comments from members of two core subject departments will serve to illustrate this point:

> Both *the extremely able and the least able students* would fit into that category [that is 'special needs'], and on the whole the extremely able tend not to be catered for separately in this school, until [the new coordinator] arrived.

> [The term 'special needs' applies to] children in the normal distribution in *the bottom 5 per cent and the top 5 per cent.*

The teachers concerned were members, respectively, of the English and mathematics departments; it will be recalled that the subcultures of these two departments stood in contrast to one another, the English department moving to favour forms of provision associated with the discourse of inclusion (for example mixed ability groupings), the mathematics department acting as a bastion of the discourse of deviance (for example in placing pupils in ability sets). Another theoretical definition of 'special needs' was offered by a member of staff who taught French and PE, and also held pastoral responsibilities as a head of year. It will be recalled that the modern foreign languages department, like the mathematics department, was committed to the policy of setting, a position which was defended by this interviewee. However, in discussing her understanding of 'special needs', she stressed the multi-dimensional nature of the concept, explaining that in her pastoral role, in contrast to the point of view of the subject teacher, she had to think of 'the whole child', a perspective which encompassed educational, social, behavioural and emotional needs and difficulties. She went on:

> I see special needs as being a problem which could occur to every child in a school at any time. . . . You have to cater for *the less able and the most able* . . . [There are] two categories of special need . . . serious special needs, which are an ongoing thing, and we have others which appear now and

again and maybe just last a couple of weeks, and maybe these are the ones that sometimes we don't tackle early enough, due to lack of information. . . . I teach PE and French and I have to tackle special needs very differently . . . *special needs isn't just one thing.*

This account suggests a sophisticated, multi-layered understanding of the term 'special needs'. The teacher's comments identify a variety of factors which may be implicated in the occurrence of difficulties in learning, and a range of dimensions along which they can vary, including: ability (again, embracing the most and least able pupils); affect; duration; severity; and the area of the curriculum in question. These examples show that, in spite of major variations in the subculture of departments, and associated differences in orientation towards the prevailing organization of provision, there could be a degree of overlap in the formal definition of the key term 'special needs' articulated within the divergent discourses. In accounting for the common shift in thinking among teachers whose professional outlooks otherwise differed considerably, it seems likely that an important factor was the character of the school's intake, which, by general consent, contained a high proportion of pupils who were expected to succeed academically. In any event, the theoretical overlap between the discourses over this issue constituted a favourable ground for the drive to develop provision for able students, which was led by the coordinator as a means to enhancing the differentiation of the curriculum.

Prescribing different trajectories of development – conflict postponed?

Notwithstanding the areas of working compromise and theoretical overlap described above, it remained the case that the discourses parted company over a number of concrete issues which were of long-term significance for the development of provision in the school. The contradiction between them was most evident over the questions of the role of support teaching, and the value of teachers' professional development. As I have illustrated above, the discourse of deviance envisaged teaching support in terms of the provision of direct teaching assistance in the classroom, and saw the possession of specialist subject knowledge on the part of the teacher as crucial to the effectiveness of such support. Similarly, within this discourse, doubt was cast on the value of 'INSET' activities aimed at developing teachers' skills, whilst practical wisdom accrued from classroom experience was seen as being at the heart of a teacher's professional expertise. By contrast, central to the model of support for learning put forward in the discourse of inclusion was the concept of collaborative curriculum development work, which would take place predominantly at the planning stage, and was seen to require generic skills in differentiation rather than specialist subject knowledge; direct support teaching in the classroom, on the other hand, was not seen to be effective as a major strategy of provision. Furthermore, within this discourse, central importance was attached to the continuing professional development of all teaching staff as a means of improving the presentation of the curriculum across the school; stress was laid upon the need for teachers to be engaged in a continuous process of developing and updating their professional skills, rather than relying on their established practice. It seems clear that these disagreements were of fundamental significance, since if put into practice they would prescribe very different trajectories of development for the school; they carried practical implications for the organization of provision in the here and now (such as the role of support teachers), and for priorities in the future investment of time and resources (such as the amount and type of staff development activities).

As noted before, there was little evidence of open conflict between the two discourse constituencies over these issues at the time of the study. This may be accounted for by the fact that the coordinator, who was spearheading many of the new initiatives, had only recently been appointed to the school, and that therefore, as she put it, 'a lot of staff, because I'm new, still haven't got a clue where they stand.' For these reasons, drawing a dichotomy between dominant and subordinate discourses is not appropriate to the situation at Sealey Cove when the study took place. There was rather a sense of jockeying for position between one discursive perspective which was oriented towards creating a climate in favour of major organizational reform (the discourse of inclusion), and a contending perspective which was oriented towards a defence of the organizational *status quo ante*. The discourse of inclusion constructed a narrative of the school in which the present was seen as too much shaped by the legacy of an unsatisfactory past, and the future was envisaged in terms of a radical departure from, and improvement on, the existing state of affairs. In the narrative constructed through the discourse of deviance, on the other hand, if there were reasons to grumble about the present, it was because it was not enough like the past, when a rational pattern of provision was established, which threatened to be upset by recent innovations; consequently, the future was envisaged as a struggle to defend this threatened heritage against ill-considered proposals for radical change. There is a close analogy between this pattern of relationships and the distinction between young 'innovators' and the 'old guard' made by Ball (Ball 1987) in his discussion of 'intergenerational conflict' in schools, though in this case the dividing line was not so much between older and younger teachers as between long-stay and recently appointed staff. Also, in Sealey Cove, as has been mentioned, it was too early to say that battle had been joined in earnest between the opposing points of view. However, the discourse of inclusion was in the ascendant within the school, in the sense that it was setting the agenda for institutional development; the outlook which it embodied was in harmony with the vision of powerful members of staff (including members of the senior management team) with authority to make decisions which would shape the school's development, such as staff appointments and budget allocations. By contrast, the discourse of deviance was on the defensive, and was increasingly obliged to react to school development initiatives proposed by supporters of the discourse of inclusion, rather than itself setting the pace of events or the agenda for debate within the school's professional culture. The discourse of inclusion was thus better positioned at the time of the study to influence the future development of the school.

CHAPTER FIVE

Pedagogical discourse: a theoretical model

My aim in this chapter is to theorize the concept of pedagogical discourse. I use this term to signify an interconnected set of beliefs held by a constituency of teaching staff in a common institutional setting about the nature, purposes and methods of education which combine to make up a working theory of schooling. The model I propose here is based on the evidence of case studies of two English secondary schools where initiatives were under way to develop more inclusive forms of provision. However, in this chapter, I seek to abstract from the contingencies of these particular schools, in order to build a general model which may help to elucidate the issues at stake in other settings where comparable initiatives are being considered. In the sense in which the term is used here, therefore, 'discourse' refers not only to the vocabulary that teachers use to describe their work, but more fundamentally to the underlying grammar of reasoning which can be inferred from their comments on the current organization of provision in the school, and possible changes to that organization which they desire or fear. It is a means of accounting for institutional policy and practice from a definite evaluative standpoint, of defining its present state against a normative conception of what it might be or ought to be.

My analysis of the evidence from the case studies leads me to suggest that two contrasting forms of pedagogical discourse, generally articulated by different constituencies of staff, can be identified; I call these the discourse of deviance and the discourse of inclusion. They can be distinguished along a number of dimensions, which are summarized in Table 5.1.

In what follows, I will take each discourse in turn, starting with the discourse of deviance, and seek to elaborate on these dimensions by constructing a social history of the perspective which they represent.

Table 5.1   Two forms of pedagogical discourse

Dimension	Discourse of deviance	Discourse of inclusion
Educability of students	There is a hierarchy of cognitive ability on which students can be placed	Every student has an open-ended potential for learning
Explanation of educational failure	The source of difficulties in learning lies in deficits of ability which are attributes of the student	The source of difficulties in learning lies in insufficiently responsive presentation of the curriculum
School response	Support for learning should seek to remediate the weaknesses of individual students	Support for learning should seek to reform curriculum and develop pedagogy across the school
Theory of teaching expertise	Expertise in teaching centres in the possession of specialist subject knowledge	Expertise in teaching centres in engendering the active participation of all students in the learning process
Curriculum model	An alternative curriculum should be provided for the less able	A common curriculum should be provided for all students

The discourse of deviance

A view of students' capacity to learn would seem to be fundamental to any theory of education. One point of departure which educators may adopt for their thinking on this question is a view of students' educability as bounded and circumscribed by inherent limitations, arising from a substratum of (essentially fixed) cognitive ability. This view has a long history, and undoubtedly exerted a powerful influence on the shape of the school system in Britain during the twentieth century. For most of this period, a proportion of children of school age were officially deemed to be ineducable, that is incapable of benefiting from educational provision in schools. Shortly after the introduction of compulsory schooling, the Elementary Education (Defective and Epileptic Children) Act 1899 adopted the concept of mental deficiency, and instituted a regime of medical examination to identify defective children, who were to be excluded from elementary schools (Copeland 1999). (Some attended separate special schools, though up to the end of World War 2 such provision was far from universally available.) The 1944 Education Act introduced a legal distinction between the educable and ineducable and established ten statutory categories of handicap. Children deemed to be educationally subnormal were to be sent to special treatment centres, administered by the health authorities. Only with the passing of the Education (Handicapped Children) Act in 1970 was responsibility for these centres transferred to Local Education Authorities. This could be taken to mark the end of a distinction in law between educable and ineducable children, though the categories of handicap remained on the statute book for a further decade until the 1981 Education Act replaced them with the concept of special educational needs. The term 'ineducable' is no longer found in contemporary education policy, though it could be argued that its echoes continue to reverberate in the notion that children with learning difficulties require special educational provision, which is 'additional to, or otherwise different from' that which is generally made for children of the same age in local schools, a definition introduced in the 1981 Act and in continuing use since then (DFEE 2000; DFES 2001).

An important ideological buttress for the concept of ineducability and the series of policy settlements which it informed was provided by intelligence quotient (IQ) theory. This originated in the work of the French psychologist Binet, who sought to develop a method of identifying children who needed extra help to progress in school. In the 1920s and 1930s his work was picked up by American psychologists influenced by the ideas of the eugenics movement (Rose et al. 1984). Already committed to a view of intelligence as fixed and innate, in their hands IQ tests became a tool to provide ostensibly scientific data in support of this outlook; their research was used to justify policies such as the compulsory sterilization of 'idiots' in many states, and the 1924 Immigration Restriction Act which was framed to keep out southern Europeans on the grounds of purportedly inferior intelligence (Gould 1981). IQ theory was further developed in Britain by Sir Cyril Burt, the most influential of the early educational psychologists, who also promoted a hereditarian view of intelligence. Burt's work has since been discredited, for it is clear that between the 1940s and the 1970s he reported statistical correlations, supposed to demonstrate the heritability of IQ, which remained so unchanging as to be wildly improbable (Rose et al. 1984). Indeed, it seems that his later publications should be judged against the canons of fiction rather than of research, since it is doubtful that he carried out any of the empirical studies which they report. Whilst it would be a mistake to describe Burt as the architect of the 11-plus examination, the psychological movement of which he was part underpinned the view of differential educability on which the system of selective secondary education, introduced by the 1944 Education Act, was based (a system which continues to be operated in a number of predominantly Conservative boroughs in England to this day). In general, we can say that there is a historical affinity between the view that students' educability is fundamentally circumscribed by a global, determinate intellectual capacity and policy regimes which construct a differentiated system of schooling, in which some students are denied access to high-status forms of provision.

The idea that intelligence is a fixed, innate quantity distributed among the population in a normal curve carries with it a ready-made explanation for the manifest phenomenon of educational failure, viz. that the root cause lies in an underlying lack of ability on the part of the student. As I argued in Chapter 1, this 'individual deficit' model has been particularly influential in the psycho-medical tradition of research into learning difficulties, resulting in a preoccupation with speculative aetiologies and the elaboration of increasingly refined taxonomies of syndrome subtypes, often of little apparent educational consequence. There have, however, been other attempts to explain differential patterns of educational achievement which do not rely on a biological determinist view of intelligence, but which nevertheless entail a student-deficit outlook. One of the most enduring of these is cultural deprivation theory. Whilst its roots can be traced back to Victorian social reformism, this sociological theory became particularly influential in the 1960s, as an attempt to account for the stubborn persistence of inequalities in educational outcomes, especially between children from working class and middle class families, in an era when economic expansion and an allied extension of higher education coincided with a dominant ideology of meritocracy. The theory assumed various forms, the origins of the cultural deficits ascribed to working class children being accounted for in terms of parental attitudes (Douglas 1964), a preference for immediate as opposed to deferred gratification (Schneider and Lysgaard 1953; cited in Banks 1971), or the habitual use of a restricted (rather than an elaborated) speech code (Bernstein 1975). It also exercised a significant influence on policy initiatives such as Operation Headstart in the US and Educational Priority Areas in the UK. These programmes of compensatory education were designed to make good the cultural deficits which children from disadvantaged backgrounds were thought to suffer from, but generally failed to close the attainment gap in the way that policy-makers had forecast. Whilst underresourcing played a part in the failure of these initiatives, there are deeper problems with the idea of cultural deprivation itself on which they were largely based. First, it is difficult to see how cultural deprivation theory can account for the fact that, whilst the educational attainments of working class children are systematically lower than those of middle class children, some working class children do succeed educationally. Second, this outlook tends to treat the dominant values and norms in society in an uncritical fashion, presupposing that the characteristics of middle class culture are by definition desirable. Yet in capitalist economies, access to high-status, well-paid jobs is always limited, determined not by the output of the education system, but by the structure of the labour market. It is not clear why the prospect of dedicating oneself to a lengthy educational career in pursuit of ever higher credentials should be expected to appeal equally to all, when the organization of the economy means that entry to professional and managerial positions is inevitably confined to a minority. Finally, in ascribing the cause of educational failure to factors in the student's home background, cultural deprivation theory legitimates the current institutional organization of schools, which is not seen as implicated in the production of that failure. Present Government policy in the UK, for example, favours the increased use of setting arrangements in secondary and primary schools, despite the well-established finding of educational research that such internal hierarchies within the school create a subculture of alienation and disaffection among students placed in the lower groups (Hargreaves 1967).

Individual pathology accounts of educational failure gave rise to a specific form of institutional response, the tradition of remedial education, which was the dominant model of provision for students with learning difficulties in mainstream schools in the UK between the 1950s and the 1970s. As the name indicates, this approach was founded on an analogy with clinical practice in medicine, suggesting that a certain proportion of children could be identified in schools whose performance was below what might be expected owing to some individual weakness or deficiency, which might be corrected by a proper course of treatment. Underpinning this notion was the distinction drawn by psychologists between various gradations of mental deficiency, and in particular that made by Burt and others between the innately dull, who could not be expected to benefit from remedial intervention, and the 'backward' or 'retarded' child who could (Burt 1937; Schonell 1942). Remedial education was a somewhat elastic concept which covered a variety of specific arrangements, but in practice most students who fell within its orbit were withdrawn or extracted from the mainstream curriculum for varying amounts of time to receive separate teaching in the basic skills, that is literacy, especially reading, and arithmetic. The rationale for this was that these skills were prerequisites for participation in the rest of the curriculum – children needed to attain a certain minimum level of competence in these areas before it was possible for them to make progress in history, geography or physics, for example. By withdrawing 'backward' children from some of the regular subject timetable, they could receive intensive coaching from a teacher with specialist expertise in the teaching of the basic skills, until they reached the requisite level of ability in these areas, when they could return to the mainstream curriculum on a full-time basis. Unfortunately this theory was rarely very effective in practice. Many of those who were drawn into the remedial system stayed there throughout their school career, and spent an increasing proportion of their time withdrawn from mainstream lessons as they progressed through the school; often there was a blurring of boundaries between remedial provision and the 'bottom set' in the secondary school. As a result, these students frequently experienced a narrow, impoverished curriculum which exposed them to a repetitive diet of mechanical exercises in comprehension and arithmetic; and of course, the more work they missed in the mainstream curriculum, the further behind they slipped compared with the rest of their peers, and the less likely they were to be able to make a successful return to full-time participation in regular subject lessons. A second effect of the remedial approach was that it tended to deflect attention from the selective nature of the mainstream curriculum itself. The internal division of labour within the school between high-status subject teaching and low-status remedial work served to reinforce the belief that the subject teacher's job was to impart the specialist knowledge of their discipline to those students capable of absorbing it, rather than to concern themselves with adapting their materials or teaching style to accommodate students' diverse starting points and current capabilities. It is no accident that the great growth period of remedial education in the 1960s coincided with the curtailment of selection and the rise of comprehensive secondary education. Within the newly-established comprehensive schools, the remedial system performed a dual function: it answered the need of former grammar school teachers to protect the academic prestige of their subject discipline; and it provided a niche for some former secondary modern school teachers, whose work with 'non-academic' students, while less prestigious, could nevertheless be presented as essential if the smooth running of the subject departments was to continue. Remedial education, then, entrenched a permanent state of emergency in the institutional structure of secondary schools, providing as critics remarked 'an ambulance service in a system which was prone to accident' (Golby and Gulliver 1979: 142), but thereby also tending to legitimate the unreconstructed mainstream curriculum which was the source of its clients.

The decade following the Warnock Report (DES 1978) and the 1981 Education Act saw a growing movement of self-criticism and questioning within the professional remedial education community and a steady shift of opinion in favour of a new model of school-level policy known as the 'whole school approach' to special educational needs (Bines 1986; Dessent 1987). Once again, this concept contained an inherent vagueness which meant that it could be used to describe various forms of provision, but it came to be defined in contrast to remedial education as signifying a de-emphasizing of the practice of withdrawal and an increase in the use of in-class support teaching, combined with a stress on the need to 'differentiate' the curriculum, that is to adapt resources and teaching methods to suit the range of ability which, it was argued, is found in any group of students. The shifting consensus among the community of practitioners was symbolized by the formation of the National Association for Special Educational Needs (NASEN) in 1992 when the National Association for Remedial Education (NARE) amalgamated with the National Council for Special Education (NCSE). For the new 'special needs' community, the concept of the whole school approach also signified a relocation of responsibility for teaching students with difficulties, who were no longer to be removed for treatment by the special educational needs department, but were to remain in mainstream subject lessons, with subject departments primarily responsible for ensuring their continued educational progress. Concomitantly, the role of the special educational needs coordinator was to be defined increasingly in terms of managing an area of cross-curricular provision and supporting the work of subject teachers through consultation, advice and joint work on differentiating the curriculum, but not for the most part in terms of providing direct, face-to-face tuition for a minority of problematic students (Gains 1994). The extent to which these aims were realized in practice, however, did not depend solely on the efforts of special needs coordinators. The concept of the whole school approach emerged in a context where the entire school curriculum and the working conditions of all teaching staff were being powerfully reshaped by the neo-liberal policies of the Thatcher Government, most notably in the 1988 Education Reform Act which followed the abandonment of a defensive campaign of strike action by the main teaching unions in 1986–7. At the same time as imposing quasi-market mechanisms on the funding and governance of the school system, thus encouraging competition between schools for students and the units of resourcing attached to them, this Act also introduced a National Curriculum which was to become compulsory for all state-maintained schools. The National Curriculum comprised a set of ten subjects, stratified into three 'core' subjects (English, mathematics and science) which were to be prioritized on the timetable and remain obligatory for all students up to the age of 16, and seven additional subjects which had to compete for space on the remaining 50 per cent of the timetable, some of which became optional from the age of 14 (art, history, geography, modern foreign languages, music, physical education and technology). Attainment targets were also set out specifying the knowledge and skills which students of a particular age group were expected to have acquired, and a national system of testing introduced using standard assessment tasks (SATs); the results of these tests were collated and published to produce league tables of school performance. At the same time as subject teachers were being exhorted to 'differentiate' in response to students' varying levels of prior knowledge and understanding, therefore, an essentialist model of the curriculum was being promulgated, framed in terms of fixed academic content knowledge and an expectation of linear progression in learning by the majority of students; and where average test scores fell below these benchmarks, schools were publicly branded as 'failing' by the newly-privatized schools inspectorate (OFSTED) and by education ministers. In these circumstances, it is scarcely surprising if the notion of a shared responsibility for the education of students with difficulties in learning received a less than wholehearted welcome from subject teaching departments. Whilst there was undoubtedly a general reduction in the use of extraction in secondary schools in the 1990s, this was accompanied by a continuing nostalgia for remedial provision from a section of subject teachers, and as the case studies presented in Chapters 3 and 4 show, the desirability of a whole school, as opposed to a remedial, approach remained a live issue in staffrooms in this period. Other teachers saw the ideal solution to the differentiation/standardization dilemma as an ever-increasing use of in-class support teaching and assistance targeted on individually-identified students. In questioning this view, I do not mean to doubt the efficacy of individual support in enabling student participation in particular circumstances, but rather to suggest that relying on this as a regular strategy of first resort carries with it the danger of creating a dependency in the students targeted, and of reinforcing their 'apartness' in the classroom. Unless in-class support teaching is carefully planned and based on a collaborative working relationship between staff, there is a risk that it ends by replicating remedial provision within the classroom.

The introduction of the National Curriculum also acted as a powerful reinforcement for a particular view of pedagogical expertise, namely that it centres primarily in the possession of specialist subject knowledge. This image of schoolteaching was not of course created by the National Curriculum, being part of the heritage of the grammar school tradition carried by the secondary sector, with the prestige it attached to membership of an academic discipline. It had long been embedded in the organizational structure of secondary schools, founded for the most part on the strong internal division between subject departments, which form the 'home' within the school to which most teaching staff belong, and the terrain on which the micropolitics of decisions about staffing levels and allocation of budgets are conducted. Historical studies of the development of the school curriculum have also shown how advocates of new areas of study (for example geography, biology) have regularly been driven to formulate syllabi which emphasize abstract, academic know-ledge in order to compete with the established, respectable subject disciplines (Goodson 1993). Nevertheless, there have been periodic attempts to challenge this tradition, and the early years of comprehensive education in particular saw a series of local experiments aimed at loosening the boundaries between subject departments and the domains of knowledge which they encode. Examples included initiatives to establish integrated humanities courses, reorganization of departments into broader faculty groupings, and alternative approaches to timetabling, such as the use of an 'integrated day' in the early years of secondary schooling, designed to promote increased interdisciplinary collaboration between staff and a more holistic curricular experience for stu-dents. Some of these experiments continued into the 1980s, but the more radical forms of restructuring were largely abandoned as impossible to manage after the introduction of the National Curriculum, which contained not just a stratification of knowledge into subject areas, but an implicit model of the structure of the school timetable expressed in terms of the proportion of time which students should spend studying particular subjects. The precise detail of timetable organization remained the local responsibility of the school, but the National Curriculum placed very strong constraints on its architecture, which discouraged radical departures from a subject-led design. A narrow subject-specialist view of teaching expertise was further promulgated in the 1990s by the Teacher Training Agency, established by the 1994 Education Act. In 1998 the Agency issued a series of documents which set out the knowledge, under-standing, skills and attributes required of teachers at various stages of career progression (TTA 1998a, 1998b). These National Standards replaced more gen-eral competences and consistently prioritized specialist subject knowledge as the defining characteristic of the secondary teacher's expertise; in the stan-dards for the award of qualified teacher status, for example, 14 different items of knowledge and understanding are listed in the opening section of the document, each of which reiterates the concept of subject specialism. These tendencies seemed likely to be further reinforced by the New Labour Govern-ment's determination to impose performance-related pay on the teaching pro-fession, which tied an element of teachers' pay to the scores attained by their students in standard national tests. Government guidance on threshold standards and performance management again stressed subject knowledge and monitoring of pupil progress by SATs results in the subject area as key criteria against which headteachers and governors should judge the eligibility of staff for pay increases. This policy thus contained a material incentive to strengthen the boundaries between subject departments in secondary schools and discourage cross-curricular collaboration among staff.

Proponents of the National Curriculum claimed that one of its beneficial consequences would be an end to the notion of an 'alternative curriculum' associated with the remedial education tradition, which saw a minority of students denied access to high-status areas of knowledge and learning, and offered instead a mixture of basic skills work and non-academic activities. It is true that its introduction imposed a greater formal uniformity on the expected content of the curriculum than had previously been the case, and made it more difficult for schools to justify syphoning off a proportion of students to spend most of their time on non-examined courses. However, it would be a mistake to examine the National Curriculum in isolation in this regard, for its framework was overlaid upon a context defined by the prior expansion of programmes of pre-vocational education in the mid-1980s, such as the Technical and Vocational Education Initiative (TVEI) and the Certificate of Pre-Vocational Education (CPVE). These programmes were sponsored by the then Conservative Government in response to concerns about the social tensions created by spiralling levels of youth unemployment which were a consequence of its economic policies. Whilst the specific initiatives were superseded, a general split in the post-14 curriculum remained between the minority of 'academic' students deemed to be candidates for higher education, and the majority who were expected either to leave formal education at 16, or to be destined for more vocationally-oriented courses of further education. At 14, students must choose their 'option' subjects and are assigned to teaching groups in preparation for the General Certificate of Secondary Education (GCSE) examinations at 16, and it is at this point that a formal differentiation between the academic and non-academic groups typically takes place. However, the system of national testing at earlier ages (7, 11 and 14), combined with the Government policy of encouraging greater use of setting by ability in the primary sector, might be thought to be driving this process of differentiation further and further back through the education system. The formal uniformity of the National Curriculum and its prescribed expectations for levels of attainment by students at particular ages may conceal a reality in which the reach of institutionalized processes of differentiation is extended backwards, shaping the child's experience of schooling in an increasingly powerful way from the beginning of their educational career.

The discourse of inclusion

The findings of the case studies reported in Chapters 3 and 4 indicated that a second major perspective on the goals, purposes and methods of education could be identified which was generally articulated by a different constituency of staff within the schools investigated, and which diverged systematically from the discourse of deviance along the dimensions set out in Table 5.1. I call this the discourse of inclusion. In this section, I aim to elaborate on the premises of the discourse as presented in the table by anchoring them in critical educational theory and outlining their implications for the development of school policy and pedagogical practice. I argued above that the influence of the assumptions associated with the discourse of deviance could be traced in various aspects of educational policy in Britain during the twentieth century. However, these assumptions did not go unchallenged, and it may be helpful to think of the discourse of inclusion as an alternative vision of the relationship between education and society which runs counter to the hegemonic processes of segregation and differentiation that have dominated the historical development of mass schooling; a vision which had a partial impact on particular moments of policy development in the past, such as the general shift from selective to comprehensive secondary schools in the 1960s and 1970s, and which suggests a specific orientation towards contemporary policy initiatives.

The critical demolition of IQ theory which was described above gave rise to a number of attempts to provide alternative definitions of the concept of intelligence which avoided the pitfalls of hereditarian notions, such as Holt's view that 'the true test of intelligence is not how much we know, but how we behave when we don't know what to do' (Holt 1982: 271), or Giddens's ironic reflection that intelligence is what intelligence tests measure (Giddens 1997). However, with regard to efforts to develop a unified, comprehensive educational system capable of promoting the learning of all students, the term seems so mired in biological determinist assumptions that it is better to dispense with it altogether and look for an alternative way of conceptualizing educability which does not depend on the notion that individuals can be assigned a natural rank defined by a fixed mental capacity supposed to be inherited at birth. A theoretical source for such an approach can be found in the tradition of socio-cultural psychology originating in the work of Vygotsky and his followers who were active in the Soviet Union in the 1920s and 1930s, and whose work was rediscovered by Western scholars in the 1960s (Vygotsky 1934/1986; Vygotsky 1978). Vygotsky posits that all specifically human learning arises from the internalization of social relationships; mind is an emergent property of verbal interaction, and our capacity for conscious thought, reasoning and reflection – all the faculties conventionally associated with the term 'intelligence' – can be understood as a form of inner speech. (There are many points of contact between Vygotsky's position and the social constructionist theory of mind developed independently by Mead in the US in the first decades of the twentieth century (Mead 1934).) Vygotsky puts forward the following statement of the 'law of cultural development':

> An interpersonal process is transformed into an intrapersonal one. Every function in the child's cultural development appears twice: first, on the social level, and later, on the individual level; first, between people (interpsychological), and then inside the child (intrapsychological). . . . All the higher functions originate as actual relations between human individuals.
>
> (Vygotsky 1978: 57)

It will be seen that this view of psychological development is radically incompatible with a belief in intelligence as a fixed, biologically-given quantity (the so-called 'g' factor or general intelligence hypothesized in IQ theory). For Vygotsky, individuation (the development of the psyche) is coextensive with socialization (becoming a member of a cultural community). The architecture of the mind is a function of the quality of social interaction from which the experience of selfhood is constituted. And crucially, Vygotsky's formulation suggests an open-ended, not a closed view of the course of individual development, for if the self is fashioned out of the social experience of relationships with others, then there can be no ceiling to potential development which is predetermined on the basis of heredity.

This view of the socio-cultural origin of mind led Vygotsky to propose another theoretical concept, the celebrated 'zone of proximal development', which sheds new light on the distinctively human capacity for learning under deliberate instruction mediated by linguistic interaction. He defines the zone of proximal development in the following terms:

the distance between the actual developmental level as determined by independent problem solving and the level of potential development as determined through problem solving under adult guidance or in collaboration with more capable peers.

(Vygotsky 1978: 86)

Unlike the conventional notion of intelligence, the zone of proximal development is not to be seen as the fixed attribute of an individual, but as a property of the dynamic relationship between members of a social collective who are differently positioned by virtue of their previous experience of participating in the life of the community. It is a measure of the difference between the individual subject's current independent competence in a given sphere of activity and the greater degree of proficiency which is within their reach when working in collaboration with others more experienced than themselves; between what she/he can presently do on their own and what they can accomplish with informed help. In a useful analogy, this has been described as an 'apprenticeship' model of learning (Rogoff 1990) for, whilst Vygotsky in his own work concentrated largely on the fields of child development, school education and learning disabilities, it is clear that the general conceptual framework he put forward can be extended to the study of other areas such as adult education and occupational learning; indeed, his analysis suggests that the kind of mentoring partnership which was often established as a way of inducting new workers into the production process in early industrial societies (apprenticeship) can be used as a way of conceptualizing learning under many other circumstances – we learn through guided participation in joint productive activity in institutionalized cultural settings. From the point of view of childhood education, this outlook also led Vygotsky to reject the idea of 'readiness' for learning associated with the psychology of Piaget and his theory of a set sequence of maturationally-determined stages of development. Against this, Vygotsky argued that 'the only "good learning" is that which is in advance of development' (Vygotsky 1978: 89), that is that the human capacity for deliberate tuition involves a certain 'forcing' of the pace of unaided development which can call forth new psychological processes, expanding the range of 'thinking tools' available to the child and accelerating the growth of the mind (for example, by demonstrating the use of linguistic techniques to facilitate memory as in mnemonic strategies). Finally, we may note that the concept of the zone of proximal development is future-oriented, stressing potential and the open-ended, unfinalized nature of the self in contrast to the view of the individual's identity as circumscribed by innate limitations projected by IQ theory. As Vygotsky puts it, 'what a child can do with assistance today she will be able to do by herself tomorrow' (Vygotsky 1978: 87).

The Vygotskian tradition thus marks a decisive rejection of hereditarian theories of intelligence. From the point of view of the socio-cultural understanding of mind, it is not so much that the biological determinist approach is empirically mistaken or overestimates the influence of heredity versus environment in this area, as that it is a defunct research programme which sets out to study a non-existent object. Our biology defines certain physical characteristics which mark us anatomically as a species (such as a skeletal frame adapted to bipedalism), but it is culture which makes us human. As Vygotsky pointed out, all specifically human forms of learning are mediated through cultural systems which have a historical origin, the most important being the social semiotic system of language. Our ability to use language, including the silent language of thought, to guide our activity, to plan, reflect, and formulate a sense of purpose – all those faculties which distinguish us from other animal species and are conventionally referred to by the term 'intelligence' – is not a genetically given function at all, but a skill learnt through the experience of participating in social interaction in definite cultural settings. It follows that, where the course of learning is impeded, the explanation is not to be sought in our genes, which are presumably refractory to any educative labour, but in remediable features of the culture we inhabit. IQ theory and the notion of inherited intelligence in general constitute a pseudo-scientific ideology which functions to legitimate the systematic reproduction of social inequality and to deter enquiry into the reformable conditions of schooling which are implicated in the production of differential patterns of educational attainment. The socio-cultural theory of mind, by contrast, orients us to consider and act to change the nexus of institutionalized relationships which contrive to produce mass educational failure.

Where the discourse of deviance ascribes difficulties in learning to individual pathology, then, the open-ended view of educability associated with the discourse of inclusion directs attention instead to the quality of the human relationship between the tutor and the learner, and invites us to reflect on the contribution that aspects of school organization, curriculum and pedagogy make to producing student failure and disaffection. I noted above, for example, how the bureaucratic organizational structure of secondary schools, with their sharply-defined internal boundaries between subject departments, militated against flexible, collaborative working arrangements between staff and made it more difficult to secure the diffusion of creative, innovative responses to student diversity across the school as a whole. The hardening of internal divisions within the school was reinforced by the essentialist model of the curriculum embedded in the 1988 Education Act and subsequent modifications, which defined the curriculum in terms of a fixed body of academic content knowledge which could be set out in an authoritative written formulation, in advance of any particular encounter between a teacher and a group of students, thus perpetuating the image of schools as 'museums of culture' (Giroux 1997). Also built into the framework of the National Curriculum is a regime of standardized testing containing an anticipation of lockstep progression on the part of most students which necessarily pathologizes those who fail to attain the prescribed targets at the required moment in their school career. If schools are to become more responsive to student diversity, then a reconceptualization of the curriculum is needed which recognizes its enacted nature, that is that a curriculum is brought to life only in the relationship built up over time between a teacher and a group of students. The work of curriculum development, therefore, should start not from the abstract end-point of prescribed knowledge to be acquired, but from the concrete starting-point of the present state of students' knowledge and understanding, the aim of instruction being to build a bridge between what students already know how to do independently and the new level of understanding and proficiency which it lies within their reach to achieve with the aid of the teacher. If their experience of education is to increase their ability to direct their own learning over time and enable them to become less reliant on the intervention of the teacher, then it would also seem necessary that the presentation of the curriculum should permit students to exercise a measure of negotiated choice over their own activity, since without this they will be confined to a relationship of dependence and denied the opportunity to demonstrate the autonomy that they are capable of. Whilst a range of teaching methods and forms of student participation would continue to be supported under this approach to developing the curriculum, it is likely that it would favour a general increase in the use of group enquiry activities, as a means of stimulating curiosity and enabling students to learn by taking an active part in the collective task of knowledge production, as opposed to the ritualistic exchanges or mere passivity often generated by didactic, transmission-based styles of pedagogy. Such an approach seeks to harness the rich resource for learning which the reality of student diversity makes available (Booth et al. 2000), and to exploit the combined talents of different individuals to the common benefit of the working group, fostering a climate of cooperation in place of the destructive inter-student rivalries set up by the competitive, individualist modes of assessment used in the present regime of national testing. In addition, the sedimented practices which constitute the hidden curriculum of schooling and help to perpetuate its differentiating effects – outcomes such as the gendered nature of subject choice at GCSE or the disproportionately large number of Afro-Caribbean boys who are permanently excluded from school – these persistent patterns of structural inequality need to be exposed and critically examined as part of the unfinalized work of curriculum development involved in building an inclusive school community.

I noted above how various suggestions were put forward in the 1980s and 1990s for a reconceptualization of the task of learning support provision in reaction to the failings of the remedial education tradition – proposals for school reform such as the 'refashioned mainstream' (Gartner and Lipsky 1989) or the 'adhocratic school' (Skrtic 1991a). A number of local and district-level initiatives were established in the US and Britain in the 1990s which sought to put these ideas into practice (NCERI 1995; Jordan and Goodey 1996). One feature these models had in common was a recognition of the importance of promoting greater collaboration, flexibility and teamworking in the pattern of working relationships obtained among school staff, in line with an understanding of the curricular and pedagogic origins of difficulties in learning.

From this point of view, the primary purpose of learning support provision was seen as effecting change in the institutionalized working practices of the school in order better to tap the potential of the individual student, rather than remediating the perceived weaknesses of the individual to enable them to survive in an unchanging organizational climate – changing the school to suit the student, rather than the student to suit the school. Such initiatives sought to overcome the teacher isolationism fostered by prevailing conditions in schools, in part by encouraging more fluid forms of collaborative working between members of subject departments and 'support' teachers and challenging the traditional status difference which separated these groups. One of the conditions for the development of a more creative pedagogy was seen to be a greater pooling of the existing knowledge and expertise of staff, including a sharing of their different experiences of working with individual students, as a means of enhancing their combined ability to personalize their teaching more fully. The effort to develop a learning environment which would be better able to accommodate the diverse starting-points and talents of students, then, indicated a need to de-emphasize the prestige conventionally attached to specialist subject knowledge in the secondary sector, in favour of an understanding of pedagogical expertise centred upon engendering the active participation of the student in the learning process. It would be a mistake, though, to suppose that this understanding implied a laissez-faire approach to instruction. Researchers working in the tradition of socio-cultural learning theory proposed the metaphor of 'scaffolding' to describe the role of the tutor in enabling the construction of knowledge by less experienced learners (Wood et al. 1976), and outlined a number of specific and inalienable responsibilities which fall to the tutor in facilitating successful learning experiences. For example, it is the tutor who recruits the interest of the learner in the task to be attempted; they may have recourse to simplifying the task, or demonstrating what is to be done in an idealized form; and they may assist the learner by reminding them of what they already know which can help them to make headway in a problem-solving situation, for example by appealing to analogy with the known and familiar as a means of apprehending the new and the strange. The tutor here acts as a 'vicarious consciousness' (Bruner 1985), sharing the burden of learning with the student and reducing the complexity of the task to be mastered in order to allow the learner to concentrate on the critical features. This ability to use speech to negotiate a shared understanding of the task at hand is one of the distinctive characteristics of human learning, as Vygotsky pointed out; it is the culturally-mediated nature of human practical activity, especially its imbrication in language, that makes intentional tutoring possible.

It is equally important, however, to recognize that the relationship between tutor and learner which is envisaged in socio-cultural theory is a dynamic and interactive one, not one of fixed dependency. Pedagogy, from this point of view, aspires to the quality of 'contingent responsiveness' which also characterizes spontaneous conversation (Wells 1987), the tutor's interventions being governed by the actions and utterances of the learner, treated as evidence of their current state of understanding and of the type and amount of help they need to enable them to progress. One would also expect to see a definite direction of development in the evolution of the tutor–learner relationship over time, and in particular, a progressive 'fading' of the support provided by the tutor and an increasing transfer of responsibility to the learner for decision-making as she/he gains proficiency in a given sphere of activity (Wood and Wood 1996). A scaffolding approach to supporting learning seeks to build a shared sense of purpose and to create the feeling of security in the learner which lessens the fear of failure and encourages a willingness to take a risk, to try out something new, knowing that help is at hand if one gets stuck. But of course, we use scaffolding to aid the process of construction, not as a permanent design feature; when the building can stand on its own, we take it down. Finally in this connection, it needs to be acknowledged that Vygotsky and his followers typically treated the adult-child dyad as a paradigm for the learning process. This does not reflect the reality of life in schools, nor perhaps should it be seen as an ideal situation for all forms of learning. Other writers have proposed the idea of a 'community of enquiry' (Wells 1989) as a model for realizing the mode of learning envisaged in the socio-cultural tradition in the collective context of institutionalized educational settings (such as schools). In addition to the kind of investigative group work which was described above, strategies such as peer tutoring and cross-age tutoring offer a way of working towards this goal, since they provide an opportunity for students to cooperate in the process of knowledge generation, and to take up different discursive positions in this activity at different times, including acting in the role of tutor themselves, which in the long run may help them to gain greater metacognitive expertise in regulating their own learning: by teaching others, we learn how to teach ourselves.

I argued above that the narrowly prescriptive, content-based nature of the National Curriculum and its associated regime of standardized testing combined to create an engine of social differentiation which infiltrated the school system to its roots and reversed the levelling up of educational attainment consequent on the abolition of selective secondary schooling in the 1960s and 1970s. But I also described how the provision of an alternative curriculum favoured by the remedial education tradition frequently led to a self-fulfilling prophecy effect, in which lower-attaining students were syphoned off from the mainstream and denied access to high-status forms of knowledge, resulting in an alienating and unproductive educational career. In closing this discussion of the discourse of inclusion, it is necessary to ask whether the socio-cultural view of learning on which I have drawn is capable of supporting a definition of the curriculum which is at once common (for all) and accommodating of human difference (for each). A starting point lies in the importance, mentioned above, of shared learning experiences, including the use of strategies such as group investigations and peer tutoring, which provide opportunities for students with different talents and of different attainments to participate in the joint production of knowledge. It also seems meaningful to suggest that the citizens of a democracy could debate and formulate a policy setting forth the global goals of the education service framed in terms of providing all students with the cultural resources necessary to participate fully in the life of the community. Doubtless the specifics of any such policy would need to be kept under review, but an example might be the goal of developing critical understanding of, and productive expertise in, a range of literacies – the ability to exploit various media and secondary symbolic systems (such as writing) for one's own communicative purposes. Different students would need different kinds and amounts of help in approaching this goal (for example, learning to use a concept keyboard overlay might be useful for some but not for others), and would reach different levels of independent attainment in various modes of communication; but defining the goal in this strategic way might avoid the inherently selective nature of the detailed prescriptions of the National Curriculum subject orders (for example the order for writing at age 14 which amongst other things specifies 'knowledge of regular patterns of spelling, word families, roots of words and derivations, including stem, prefix, suffix, inflection' – a normative target which inevitably excludes a proportion of students). Related to this is the need to broaden the range of modes of student response which are sanctioned within the curriculum and assessed as valid evidence of learning, beyond the traditional reliance on written performance in competitive examinations as the defining measure of individual achievement; for example, by valuing and certificating personal contributions to collective projects as part of building a profile of each learner's development. Marx's dictum that, in a truly democratic society, 'the free development of each is the condition of the free development of all' (Marx and Engels 1848/1965: 105) could serve as a useful guiding principle for the struggle to create a unified system of comprehensive education, reminding us that the end of education is not to reduce human difference but to allow individuality to flower. However, the socio-cultural theory of mind suggests that a dialectical inversion of Marx's formulation is also necessary. The work of Vygotsky and his followers suggests that the growth of the individual personality depends on our experience of meaningful social interaction with others as participants in a common culture. From this point of view, institutionalized patterns of selection between schools, and of differentiation within them, impoverish and distort the individual development of every student, for they diminish our understanding of human difference. Participation in a diverse learning community is a prerequisite for the growth of each individual's subjectivity in all its richness; the combined development of all is the condition of the full development of each.

Bibliography

Ainscow, M. (1991a) Effective Schools for All: An Alternative Approach to Special Needs in Education, in M. Ainscow (ed.) *Effective Schools for All*. London: David Fulton.

Ainscow, M. (1991b) Towards Effective Schools for All: Some Problems and Possibilities, in M. Ainscow (ed.) *Effective Schools for All*. London: David Fulton.

Ainscow, M. (1993) *Towards Effective Schools for All*. Paper presented at the Policy Options for Special Educational Needs in the 1990s, Institute of Education, University of London.

Ainscow, M. (ed.) (1991c) *Effective Schools for All*. London: David Fulton.

Allan, J. (1996) Foucault and Special Educational Needs: a 'box of tools' for analysing children's experiences of mainstreaming, *Disability and Society*, 11(2): 219–33.

Allan, J. (1997) *Untitled paper*. Paper presented at the International seminar on 'Theoretical Perspectives on Special Education', Ålesund, Norway.

Alur, M. (2002a) Introduction, in S. Hegarty and M. Alur (eds) *Education and children with special needs: From segregation to inclusion*. New Delhi: Sage.

Alur, M. (2002b) Special Needs Policy in India, in S. Hegarty and M. Alur (eds) *Education and children with special needs: From segregation to inclusion*. New Delhi: Sage.

Armstrong, F., Armstrong, D. and Barton, L. (eds) (2000) *Inclusive Education: Policy Contexts and Comparative Perspectives*. London: David Fulton.

Avramidis, E., Bayliss, P. and Burden, R. (2002) Inclusion in action: an in-depth case study of an effective inclusive secondary school in the south-west of England, *International Journal of Inclusive Education*, 6(2): 143–63.

Ball, S.J. (1987) *The Micro-Politics of the School: Towards a Theory of School Organization*. London: Routledge.

Banerjee, R. (2002) From Integration to Inclusive Education: Seva-in-Action, in S. Hegarty and M. Alur (eds) *Education and children with special needs: From segregation to inclusion*. New Delhi: Sage.

Banks, O. (1971) *The Sociology of Education*. London: Batsford.

Bart, D.S. (1984) The Differential Diagnosis of Special Education: Managing Social Pathology as Individual Disability, in L. Barton and S. Tomlinson (eds) *Special Education and Social Interests*. London: Croom Helm.

Barton, L. (ed.) (1988) *The Politics of Special Educational Needs*. London: Falmer.

Barton, L. and Tomlinson, S. (1984a) The Politics of Integration in England, in L. Barton and S. Tomlinson (eds) *Special Education and Social Interests*. London: Croom Helm.

Barton, L. and Tomlinson, S. (eds) (1981) *Special Education: Policy, Practices and Social Issues*. London: Harper and Row.

Barton, L. and Tomlinson, S. (eds) (1984b) *Special Education and Social Interests*. London: Croom Helm.

Bernstein, B. (1975) *Class, Codes and Control (3 volumes)*. London: Routledge and Kegan Paul.

Bines, H. (1986) *Redefining Remedial Education*. London: Croom Helm.

Bloom, B.S. (ed.) (1956) *Taxonomy of Educational Objectives: The Classification of Educational Goals*. London: Longman.

Bogdan, R. and Kugelmass, J. (1984) Case Studies of Mainstreaming: a Symbolic Interactionist Approach to Special Schooling, in L. Barton and S. Tomlinson (eds) *Special Education and Social Interests*. London: Croom Helm.

Booth, T. (1996) A perspective on inclusion from England, *Cambridge Journal of Education*, 26(1): 87–99.

Booth, T. and Ainscow, M. (eds) (1998) *From Them to Us: An International Study of Inclusive Education*. London: Routledge.

Booth, T., Ainscow, M., Black-Hawkins, K., Vaughan, M. and Shaw, L. (2000) *Index for Inclusion: Developing Learning and Participation in Schools*. Bristol: CSIE.

Bowler, D.M. and Lister Brook, S. (1997) From general impairment to behavioural phenotypes: psychological approaches to learning difficulties, in M. Fawcus (ed.) *Children with Learning Difficulties: A collaborative approach to their education and management*. London: Whurr.

Bruner, J. (1985) Vygotsky: a historical and conceptual perspective, in J.V. Wertsch (ed.) *Culture, communication and cognition: Vygotskian perspectives*. Cambridge: Cambridge University Press.

Burt, C. (1937) *The Backward Child*. London: University of London Press.

Carrier, J.G. (1984) Comparative Special Education: Ideology, Differentiation and Allocation in England and The United States, in L. Barton and S. Tomlinson (eds) *Special Education and Social Interests*. London: Croom Helm.

Chib, M. (2002) Equalisation of Opportunity: What Does it Mean?, in S. Hegarty and M. Alur (eds) *Education and children with special needs: From segregation to inclusion*. New Delhi: Sage.

Clark, C., Dyson, A. and Millward, A. (eds) (1995) *Towards Inclusive Schools?* London: David Fulton.

Clark, C., Dyson, A., Millward, A. and Skidmore, D. (1995) Dialectical Analysis, Special Needs and Schools as Organizations, in C. Clark, A. Dyson and A. Millward (eds) *Towards Inclusive Schools?* London: David Fulton.

Clark, C., Dyson, A., Millward, A. and Skidmore, D. (1997) *New Directions in Special Needs: Innovations in Mainstream Schools*. London: Cassell.

Coles, G. (1987) *The Learning Mystique: A Critical Look at 'Learning Disabilities'*. New York: Pantheon.

Cooper, P. and Ideus, K. (1995) Is attention deficit hyperactivity disorder a Trojan Horse?, *Support for Learning*, 10(1): 29–34.

Copeland, I. (1995) The establishment of models of education for disabled children. *British Journal of Educational Studies*, 43(2): 179–200.

Copeland, I. (1996) The making of the dull, deficient and backward pupil in British elementary education 1870–1914, *British Journal of Educational Studies*, 44(4): 377–94.

Copeland, I. (1997) Pseudo-science and dividing practices: a genealogy of the first educational provision for pupils with learning difficulties, *Disability and Society*, 12(5): 709–22.

Copeland, I. (1999) *The Making of the Backward Pupil in England 1870–1914*. Ilford: Woburn Press.

Copeland, I.C. (1997) The Special Needs Code of Practice: antecedents and outcomes, *Cambridge Journal of Education*, 27(1): 77–92.

Corbett, J. (1996) *Bad-Mouthing: The Language of Special Needs*. London: Falmer Press.

Dasgupta, P.R. (2002) Education for the Disabled, in S. Hegarty and M. Alur (eds) *Education and children with special needs: From segregation to inclusion*. New Delhi: Sage.

DES (1978) *Special Educational Needs (The Warnock Report)*. London: HMSO.

DES (1989) *A Survey of Pupils with Special Educational Needs in Ordinary Schools*. London: DES.

DES (1990) *Provision for Primary Aged Pupils with Statements of Special Educational Needs in Mainstream Schools*. London: DES.

Dessent, T. (1987) *Making the Ordinary School Special*. London: Falmer.

DFE (1994a) *Code of Practice on the Identification and Assessment of Special Educational Needs*. London: DFE.

DFE (1994b) *The Organisation of Special Educational Provision (Circular 6/94)*. London: DFE.

DFEE (1997) *Excellence for all children: Meeting Special Educational Needs*. London: The Stationery Office.

DFEE (1998) *Meeting special educational needs: A programme of action*. Sudbury: DFEE Publications Centre.

DFEE (2000) *Draft SEN Code of Practice on the Identification and Assessment of Pupils with Special Educational Needs*. London: DFEE.

DFES (2001) *Special Educational Needs Code of Practice*. Annesley: DFES Publications.

Douglas, J.W.B. (1964) *The Home and the School: A Study of Ability and Attainment in the Primary School*. London: Panther.

DRC (2002) *Code of Practice for Schools (Disability Discrimination Act: Part 4)*. London: Disability Rights Commission.

DSA (1995) *Down's syndrome: your questions answered*. London: Down's Syndrome Association.

Dussart, G. (1994) Identifying the Clumsy Child in School: an exploratory study, *British Journal of Special Education*, 21(2): 81–6.

Dykman, R.A. and Ackerman, P.T. (1993) Behavioural Subtypes of Attention Deficit Disorder, *Exceptional Children*, 60(2): 132–41.

Fawcus, M. (ed.) (1997) *Children with Learning Difficulties: A collaborative approach to their education and management*. London: Whurr.

Freeman, A. (1988) Who's Moving the Goal Posts and What Games are We Playing Anyway: Social Competence Examined, in L. Barton (ed.) *The Politics of Special Educational Needs*. London: Falmer.

Fuchs, D. and Fuchs, L.S. (1994) Inclusive Schools Movement and the Radicalization of Special Education Reform, *Exceptional Children*, 60(4): 294–309.

Gains, C. (1994) New roles for SENCOs (Editorial), *Support for Learning*, 9(3): 102.

Gartner, A. and Lipsky, D.K. (1987) Beyond Special Education: Toward a Quality System for All Students, *Harvard Educational Review*, 57(4): 367–95.

Gartner, A. and Lipsky, D.K. (1989) New conceptualizations for special education, *European Journal of Special Needs Education*, 4(1): 16–22.

Giddens, A. (1997) *Sociology*, 3rd edn. Cambridge: Polity Press.

Giroux, H.A. (1997) *Pedagogy and the Politics of Hope: Theory, Culture and Schooling (A Critical Reader)*. Boulder, Colorado: Westview Press.

Glaser, B.G. and Strauss, A.L. (1967) *The Discovery of Grounded Theory: Strategies for Qualitative Research*. Chicago: Aldine.

Glasser, W. (1992) The Quality School, in R.A. Villa, J.S. Thousand, W. Stainback and S. Stainback (eds) *Restructuring for Caring and Effective Education: An Administrative Guide to Creating Heterogeneous Schools*. Baltimore: Paul H. Brookes.

Golby, M. and Gulliver, J.R. (1979) Whose remedies, whose ills? A critical review of remedial education, *Journal of Curriculum Studies*, 11(2): 137–47.

Goodson, I. (1993) *School Subjects and Curriculum Change: Studies in Curriculum History*, 3rd edn. (1st edn 1982). London: Falmer Press.

Gould, S.J. (1981) *The Mismeasure of Man*. London: Penguin.

Hargreaves, D.H. (1967) *Social Relations in a Secondary School*. London: Routledge and Kegan Paul.

Hart, S. (1996) *Beyond Special Needs: Enhancing Children's Learning through Innovative Thinking*. London: Paul Chapman Publishing.

Hegarty, S. (2002) Issues at the System and School Level, in S. Hegarty and M. Alur (eds) *Education and children with special needs: From segregation to inclusion*. New Delhi: Sage.

Hegarty, S. and Alur, M. (eds) (2002) *Education and children with special needs: From segregation to inclusion*. New Delhi: Sage.

Holt, J. (1982) *How Children Fail*, 2nd edn. Harmondsworth: Penguin.

Hornby, G. (1992) Integration of children with special educational needs: Is it time for a policy review?, *Support for Learning*, 7(3): 130–4.

Jordan, L. and Goodey, C. (1996) *Human rights and school change: the Newham story*. Bristol: CSIE.

Joyce, B., Murphy, C., Showers, B. and Murphy, J. (1991) School Renewal as Cultural Change, in M. Ainscow (ed.) *Effective Schools for All*. London: David Fulton.

Lister Brook, S. and Bowler, D.M. (1997) Interventions with children who have learning difficulties: contributions from clinical psychology, in M. Fawcus (ed.) *Children with Learning Difficulties: A collaborative approach to their education and management*. London: Whurr.

Marx, K. and Engels, F. (1848/1965) *The Communist Manifesto*. Moscow: Progress.

McBurnett, K., Lahey, B.B. and Pfiffner, L. (1993) Diagnosis of Attention Deficit Disorders in DSM-IV: Scientific Basis and Implications for Education, *Exceptional Children*, 60(2): 108–17.

Mead, G.H. (1934) *Mind, Self and Society*. Chicago: University of Chicago Press.

Miles, M.B. and Huberman, A.M. (1984) *Qualitative Data Analysis: A sourcebook of new methods*. Beverley Hills: Sage Publications.

Miller, D. and Mintzberg, H. (1983) The Case for Configuration, in G. Morgan (ed.) *Beyond Method: Strategies for Social Research*. London: Sage.

Millward, A. and Skidmore, D. (1995) *Local Authorities' Management of Special Needs: A Report for the Joseph Rowntree Foundation*. York: YPS.

Millward, A. and Skidmore, D. (1998) LEA responses to the management of special education in the light of the Code of Practice, *Educational Management and Administration*, 26(1): 57–66.

NCERI (1995) *National Study on Inclusion: Overview and Summary Report (National Center on Educational Restructuring and Inclusion)*. New York: The City University of New York.

Oliver, M. (1992) Intellectual masturbation: a rejoinder to Söder and Booth, *European Journal of Special Needs Education*, 7(1): 20–8.

Reid, R., Maag, J.W. and Vasa, S.F. (1993) Attention Deficit Hyperactivity Disorder as a Disability Category: A Critique, *Exceptional Children*, 60(3): 198–214.

Reid, R., Maag, J.W., Vasa, S.F. and Wright, G. (1994) Who are the Children with Attention

Deficit Hyperactivity Disorder? A School-Based Survey, *Journal of Special Education*, 28(2): 117–37.

Reynolds, D. (1991) Changing Ineffective Schools, in M. Ainscow (ed.) *Effective Schools for All*. London: David Fulton.

Reynolds, D. (1995) Using School Effectiveness Knowledge for Children with Special Needs – The Problems and Possibilities, in C. Clark, A. Dyson and A. Millward (eds) *Towards Inclusive Schools?* London: David Fulton.

Riccio, C.A., Hynd, G.W., Cohen, M.J. and Gonzalez, J.J. (1993) Neurological Basis of Attention Deficit Hyperactivity Disorder, *Exceptional Children*, 60(2): 118–24.

Rogoff, B. (1990) *Apprenticeship in Thinking: Cognitive Development in Social Context*. New York: Oxford University Press.

Rose, S., Lewontin, R.C. and Kamin, L.J. (1984) *Not in Our Genes*, 1st edn. London: Penguin.

Rouse, M. and Florian, L. (1996) Effective Inclusive Schools: a study in two countries, *Cambridge Journal of Education*, 26(1): 71–85.

Schneider, L. and Lysgaard, S. (1953) The deferred gratification pattern: a preliminary study, *American Sociological Review*, 18: 142–9.

Schön, D.A. (1983) *The Reflective Practitioner: How Professionals Think in Action*. New York: Basic Books.

Schonell, F.J. (1942) *Backwardness in the Basic Subjects*. London: Oliver and Boyd.

Sebba, J. and Ainscow, M. (1996) International Developments in Inclusive Schooling: mapping the issues, *Cambridge Journal of Education*, 26(1): 5–18.

Shulman, L.S. (1986) Those who understand: Knowledge growth in teaching. *Educational Researcher*, 15(2): 4–14.

Singh, U. (2002) Culture-Specific Paradigms of Integration in Developing Countries, in S. Hegarty and M. Alur (eds) *Education and children with special needs: From segregation to inclusion*. New Delhi: Sage.

Skidmore, D. (1996) Towards an integrated theoretical framework for research into special educational needs, *European Journal of Special Needs Education*, 11(1): 33–46.

Skidmore, D. (1997a) A dialogic pedagogy for inclusive schools. Paper presented at seminar on *Critical issues in inclusive education*, Open University, Milton Keynes, 13 June.

Skidmore, D. (1997b) Divergent pedagogical discourses and the dynamics of school culture. Paper presented at the international seminar on *Theoretical Perspectives on Special Education*, Ålesund, Norway, 25–27 May.

Skidmore, D. (1997c) Inclusion, dialogue and pedagogy. Symposium on *Need, Discipline, Support: Three discourses of schooling* held at the British Educational Research Association Conference, University of York, 11–14 September.

Skidmore, D. (1998) Pedagogical discourse and the dynamic of school development. Unpublished Ph.D. thesis, Reading University, Reading.

Skinner, B.F. (1957) *Verbal Behavior*. New York: Appleton-Century-Crofts.

Skrtic, T.M. (1991a) *Behind Special Education: A Critical Analysis of Professional Culture and School Organization*. Denver, Colorado: Love Publishing Company.

Skrtic, T.M. (1991b) Students with Special Educational Needs: Artifacts of the Traditional Curriculum, in M. Ainscow (ed.) *Effective Schools for All*. London: David Fulton.

Slee, R. (1995) *Changing Theories and Practices of Discipline*. London: Falmer Press.

Slee, R. (1996) Inclusive Schooling in Australia? Not yet!, *Cambridge Journal of Education*, 26(1): 19–32.

Slee, R. (1997) Imported or Important Theory? Sociological interrogations of disablement and special education, *British Journal of Sociology of Education*, 18(3): 407–19.

Stoll, L. (1991) School Effectiveness in Action: Supporting Growth in Schools and Classrooms, in M. Ainscow (ed.) *Effective Schools for All*. London: David Fulton.

Strauss, A. and Corbin, J. (1990) *Basics of Qualitative Research: Grounded Theory Procedures and Techniques*. Newbury Park, CA: Sage.

Strauss, A.L. (1987) *Qualitative Analysis for Social Scientists*. Cambridge: Cambridge University Press.

Thomas, G. and Loxley, A. (2001) *Deconstructing Special Education and Constructing Inclusion*. Buckingham: Open University Press.

Thousand, J.S. and Villa, R.A. (1991) Accommodating for Greater Student Variance, in M. Ainscow (ed.) *Effective Schools for All*. London: David Fulton.

Tomlinson, S. (1982) *A Sociology of Special Education*. London: Routledge and Kegan Paul.

Tomlinson, S. (1985) The Expansion of Special Education, *Oxford Review of Education*, 11(2): 157–65.

Tomlinson, S. and Colquhoun, R.F. (1995) The political economy of special educational needs in Britain, *Disability and Society*, 10(2): 191–202.

TTA (1998a) *National Standards for Qualified Teacher Status*. Chelmsford: Teacher Training Agency Publications.

TTA (1998b) *National Standards for Subject Leaders*. Chelmsford: Teacher Training Agency Publications.

Vaughan, M. (2002) International Policy and Practice in the Education of Disabled Children, in S. Hegarty and M. Alur (eds) *Education and children with special needs: From segregation to inclusion*. New Delhi: Sage.

Villa, R.A. and Thousand, J.S. (1992) Restructuring Public School Systems: Strategies for Organizational Change and Progress, in R.A. Villa, J.S. Thousand, W. Stainback and S. Stainback (eds) *Restructuring for Caring and Effective Education: An Administrative Guide to Creating Heterogeneous Schools*. Baltimore: Paul H. Brookes.

Villa, R.A., Thousand, J.S., Stainback, W. and Stainback, S. (eds) (1992) *Restructuring for Caring and Effective Education: An Administrative Guide to Creating Heterogeneous Schools*. Baltimore: Paul H. Brookes.

Vitello, S. and Mithaug, D. (eds) (1998) *Inclusive Schooling: National and International Perspectives*. Mahwah, NJ: Lawrence Erlbaum.

Vygotsky, L.S. (1934/1986) *Thought and Language* (A. Kozulin, Trans.) Cambridge, MA: MIT.

Vygotsky, L.S. (1978) *Mind in Society: The Development of Higher Psychological Processes*. Cambridge, MA: Harvard University Press.

Wang, M.C. (1991) Adaptive Instruction: An Alternative Approach to Providing for Student Diversity, in M. Ainscow (ed.) *Effective Schools for All*. London: David Fulton.

Weitzman, E.A. and Miles, M.B. (1995) *Computer Programs for Qualitative Data Analysis*. Thousand Oaks, CA: Sage.

Wells, G. (1987) *The Meaning Makers: Children Learning Language and Using Language to Learn*. London: Hodder and Stoughton.

Wells, G. (1989) Language in the classroom: literacy and collaborative talk, *Language and Education*, 3(4): 251–73.

Wood, D., Bruner, J.S. and Ross, G. (1976) The role of tutoring in problem solving. *Journal of Child Psychology and Psychiatry*, 17: 89–100.

Wood, D. and Wood, H. (1996) Vygotsky, tutoring and learning, *Oxford Review of Education*, 22(1): 5–16.

Wood, S. (1988) Parents: Whose Partners?, in L. Barton (ed.) *The Politics of Special Educational Needs*. London: Falmer.

Index

DECONSTRUCTING SPECIAL EDUCATION AND CONSTRUCTING INCLUSION

Gary Thomas and Andrew Loxley

> It should not simply be seen as an academic text for students of special education, because its relevance is much broader and its challenges to our thinking make it essential reading.
>
> TES

In this book the authors look behind special education to its supposed intellectual foundations. They find a knowledge jumble constructed of bits and pieces from Piagetian, psychoanalytic, psychometric and behavioural theoretical models. They examine the consequences of these models' influence for professional and popular thinking about learning difficulty. In turn, they explore and critique the results of this dominance for our views about children who are different and for the development of special education and its associated professions. In the light of this critique, they suggest that much of the 'knowledge' of special education is misconceived, and they proceed to advance a powerful rationale for inclusion out of ideas about stakeholding, social justice and human rights. Concluding that inclusion owes more to political theory than to psychology or sociology, the authors suggest that a rethink is needed about the ways in which we come by educational knowledge. This is important reading for students of education, and for teachers, advisers and educational psychologists.

160pp   0 335 20448 1 (Paperback)

SPECIAL EDUCATIONAL NEEDS, INCLUSION AND DIVERSITY
A TEXTBOOK

Norah Frederickson and Tony Cline

This book has the potential to become *the* textbook on special educational needs. Written specifically with the requirements of student teachers, trainee educational psychologists, SENCO's and SEN Specialist Teachers in mind, it provides a comprehensive and detailed discussion of the major issues in special education. Whilst recognising the complex and difficult nature of many special educational needs, the authors place a firm emphasis on inclusion and suggest practical strategies enabling professionals to maximise inclusion at the same time as recognising and supporting diversity.

Key features include:

- Takes full account of linguistic, cultural and ethnic diversity unlike many other texts in the field
- Addresses the new SEN Code of Practice and is completely up to date
- Recognises current concerns over literacy and numeracy and devotes two chapters to these areas of need
- Offers comprehensive and detailed coverage of major issues in special educational needs in one volume
- Accessibly written with the needs of the student and practitioner in mind

Contents
Introduction – Part one: Principles and concepts – Children, families, schools and the wider community: an integrated approach – Concepts of special educational needs – Inclusion – Special educational needs: pathways of development – Part two: Assessment in context – Identification and assessment – Reducing bias in assessment – Curriculum based assessment – Learning environments – Part three: Areas of need – Learning difficulties – Language – Literacy – Mathematics – Hearing impairment – Emotional and behaviour difficulties – Social skills – References – Index.

528pp   0 335 20402 3 (Paperback)   0 335 20973 4 (Hardback)

THE MICROPOLITICS OF INCLUSIVE EDUCATION
AN ETHNOGRAPHY

Shereen Benjamin

Shereen Benjamin's work opens up new ways of thinking about learning difficulties. This beautifully written book explores the school lives and identities of young women who find school work extraordinarily difficult for a range of reasons. It is a book to read, and read again for the rich vein of thinking about schooling and special needs that it opens up. All who are involved in teaching, policy making or school management and who are concerned about these young people should read it.

Professor Debbie Epstein, Cardiff University, UK

The drive to improve standards constructs SEN pupils as 'failing'. Yet there is a drive to educate all students within mainstream schooling i.e. 'inclusive education'. This book argues that the standards agenda in particular and its resulting impact on school policy is one of the biggest barriers to learning for SEN students. This detailed account and analysis of students' experiences of 'inclusion' in a girls' comprehensive school looks at how governmental policy initiatives – on school improvement and SEN/inclusion – are translated into practice by the school, and at how this practice is lived and understood by the girls.

176pp   0 335 21048 1 (Paperback)   0 335 21049 X (Hardback)

INCLUSIVE EDUCATION
READINGS AND REFLECTIONS

Gary Thomas and Mark Vaughan (eds)

Here, for the first time, is a book that gives some of the key ideas and streams of thought over the years that have led education in an increasingly inclusive direction. The editors draw on over 50 documents – articles, books, papers, legislation and reports – which exemplify those streams of thought, and they intersperse detailed commentary alongside the quoted extracts. Through the collection of these documents, the editors show that on principled and practical grounds there is no justification for a segregated system of schooling in the 21st century. The editors demonstrate the importance of considering equity, human rights and social justice in education. In mapping foundational changes, the book begins with Thomas Paine's *The Rights of Man* and R. H. Tawney's *Equality*, but then focuses on some landmark publications internationally over the last 40 years.

The book takes the reader on a journey that touches the historical pulse and inspiration behind progress with inclusive education, with the editors suggesting that, while the move to inclusion is slow and segregation is still widespread throughout the world, inclusion is gaining in strength. This text is for students, teachers, academics, administrators, parents and carers, voluntary organisations and politicians, and anyone else concerned with the principles, politics and practices of inclusion.

Contents
Part I: The context – rights, participation, social justice – Part II: Arguments and evidence against segregation – 1960s to today – Part III: Legislation, reports, statements – Part IV: Inclusion in action

224pp   0 335 20724 3 (Paperback)   0 335 20725 1 (Hardback)

SPECIAL TEACHING FOR SPECIAL CHILDREN
PEDAGOGIES FOR INCLUSION?

Ann Lewis and Brahm Norwich (eds)

This book addresses the question of what is special, if anything, about teaching children with special or exceptional learning needs – including pupils with low attainment, learning difficulties, language difficulties, emotional/behavioural problems or sensory needs. The answer to this question is often implied or assumed; for example, some special needs groups (e.g. dyslexia) have argued strongly for the need for particular specialist approaches. In contrast, many proponents of inclusion have argued that 'good teaching is good teaching for all' and that all children benefit from similar approaches. Both positions fail to scrutinise this issue rigorously and coherently; it is this aspect which distinguishes this book. Leading researchers in each special needs field defend and critique a conceptual analysis of the specificity of teaching strategies used with particular SEN learner groups. Summaries by the editors after each chapter link pedagogic strategies, knowledge and curriculum to key points from the chapter and pave the way for the overall discussion.

This book is indispensable reading for policy makers, researchers and professionals in the field.

Contents

How specialised is teaching pupils with disabilities and difficulties? – Deafness – Visual impairment – Deaf blindness – Severe Learning Difficulties – Profound and Multiple Learning Difficulties – Down's Syndrome – English as an additional language and speech, language and communication difficulties – Autistic spectrum disorders – AD/HD – Dyslexia – Dyspraxia – Social, emotional and behavioural difficulties – Moderate Learning Difficulties – Mixed difficulties – Overview and discussion

192pp   0 335 21405 3 (Paperback)   0 335 21406 1 (Hardback)